HELL IN A HANDBASKET

BY
SCOTT W. SCHINK

Published by:
Light Switch Press
PO Box 272847
Fort Collins, CO 80527

Copyright © 2021
ISBN: 978-1-953284-58-7
Printed in the United States of America

FOR DAD

PROLOGUE,

Every single location, institution, and person's name has been changed in the following TRUE STORY, for a host of reasons, some trivial, some legal. But the most important of these reasons, is that it does not matter the true identity's of the people that committed the crime's you are about to read about, it only matters that this story be told to the world, with the hope that just one other person on the planet, learns something from this tale, and uses that knowledge to leave this world just a little better than they found it.

AMEN

CHAPTER ONE

Imagine, if you will, what any one of North America's major urban centers is like during the month of January. Right in the dead of winter. Especially the megacities of the Great Lakes region and the northern East Coast. It is nearing the end of a brutal 2 day winter storm, inundating any one of these cities with over 18 inches of snow. Blanket of snow is a pretty good description, it literally covers EVERYTHING, there's even a bead of snow a couple of inches thick on the power lines, of all things. A very awe inspiring change, to the otherwise mundane view of the suburban skyline.

On one of these winter days, in any one of these communities, a person might overhear a New Yorker, or a Bostonian, rant and rave about all the peril's and dangers of driving in the snow.

In stark contrast, a person in California's central valley will absolutely NEVER hear a Fresnan complain about what, hands down, has to be one of worst conditions to drive in, anywhere on earth. It's a truly menacing weather phenomenon this gem of an American city suffers with each and every winter, something the people in the city of Fresno like to call "Tule Fog"

Ladies and gentlemen, this is not your run of the mill coastal fog that burns off by noon, not by a long shot. Tule fog will block out the sun for days, sometimes weeks. News reports from community's around the valley warn residents about ZERO visibility on a regular basis during the winter. How does anyone even measure ZERO visibility? I'll tell you how, you literally have to strain to see a traffic light that is just a couple of feet in front of you.

School district's here allow student's a much needed 2 hour delay for the start of classes, after which, visibility improves.

Now, those same kids that live where it snows, they are sometimes treated to what's called a "snow day". If your school had 6 or more inches of snowfall the night before, classes were cancelled for the whole day.

You never seen a happier bunch of kids in your life! Snowmen, and snowball fights, ice skating and sleigh riding, even kids making snow Angel's. A good time was had by all.

This is when a six year old boy was making a snow angel, and while he was doing so, it started snowing once again, causing William Smith to stop swinging his arms and legs. He just laid there listening, listening to a sound SO quiet, it was deaf-a-ning!!!, to this very day, it's the loudest sound he has ever heard.

CHAPTER TWO

The Barnes family lived in a two story house, a kind of cross between a southern colonial, and a mid-west farm house, with wood siding and with what was new at the time, a composition shingled roof, a pasty grey color. The house itself was a faded tan color, if there even is such a thing. Maybe it was the house itself reflecting the dullness of its occupants.

Mr. And Mrs. Barnes were not very active people and mostly kept to themselves. Their children were a little different to say the least, always racing around the neighborhood with the other neighborhood kids.

There was Jack, the oldest of the Barnes siblings, and then next in line was Bill. These brothers also had two younger sisters, Barbara first, then the youngest of the group, Eileen.

There was never much noise emanating from the Barnes household, they seemed like a normal enough of a family, maybe once or twice a year a fight between Mr. and Mrs. Barnes would be loud enough to be heard around the neighborhood.

The dynamic between the Barnes children was just like their parents, dull, and the reason for that was, weather by accident or design, 4 years separated all four siblings, which kept any of them from having anything in common. So instead of having comradery, the group had a distant kind of rivalry, and they pretty much kept to themselves. And each of them had their own interest's and talents, which meant oldest, Jack would brood over his 1/24 scale model kits.

His favorite kind to build were 18 wheeler trucks, having over a dozen in his collection.

A person could easily label Bill as the most boring of the group, keeping his nose pointed at the crease of some book, any book, novels, classics, textbooks, encyclopedias, anything he could get his hands on.

Barbara's interest and talent would make the kitchen her favorite room in the house, when it came to cooking, Barbara could easily out cook any one else in the house, including her mother.

10 year old Eileen didn't really show an interest in anything, except maybe her mother's make-up and hairspray. Eileen being the youngest, always garnered most of the attention from her parents, and that suited her just fine.

An announcement was made by Mr. And Mrs. Barnes that gave Eileen some genuine concern about that spotlight that was always pointed at her. A new brother or sister was on the way, Mr. and Mrs. Barnes were going to have another child

The attention that Eileen had become so complacent with, so dependent on for her self esteem, was waning, slowly dissipating like the stench from a smoke filled motel room when the maid comes to clean the filth from the debauchery of the night before.

CHAPTER THREE

The announcement was big news to everyone in the Barnes house, a new baby was on the way and everyone had different feelings about the impending addition to the family. Mr. Barnes now had another mouth to feed.

Two more hands to help do a bunch of chores didn't bother Jack or Barbara, who themselves were doing most of the house work, stuff their lazy, Virginia slim smoking, pill popping, mother should have been doing. In the early years of their marriage, when it was just the two boys, Mrs. Barnes didn't mind being a housewife and all the responsibility that came with it. But when her first daughter was born, her attitude towards the doting housewife role started to change. It might have been the difference between raising boys and girls. There are a lot more emotions in girls that have to be dealt with, unlike little boys, who start learning how to avoid their emotions as soon as they start having them.

It was like she just decided one day that, nope, I don't want anything else to do with this housewife crap anymore.

Bill most likely didn't care one way or the other, except that he would soon have another sister or brother to read bedtime stories to.

Eileen, on the other hand, wasn't to happy about the news of a new sibling. Everyone's excitement made Eileen realize that she wouldn't be the star attraction anymore, the family would be focused on the new baby, and most likely forget all about her. The thought of being ignored terrified Eileen, and she started to loathe the very idea of a new baby in the family.

Brooklyn, New York is the last in a string of what is called the 5 "Burroughs" of New York City. Staten Island, Manhattan, (which is considered NYC proper), Queens, The Bronx, and of course, Brooklyn. Other than Manhattan, the rest of the places on that list are basically just bedroom community's of NY,NY. And there are countless others, in just about every state bordering NY State. There's a couple in Connecticut, 1 in Rhode Island, SEVERAL in New Jersey, Vermont, New Hampshire, Pennsylvania. And upstate New York itself has Valley Stream, and Yonkers, the latter being the location of the Barnes homestead.

It was a common thing among teens and young adults during this time in the late 50's to make use of an ever expanding subway system that had great coverage of the entire New York metropolitan area. This made it possible for Barbara to visit a group of friends she had made years ago while taking some swimming lessons at a place in Brooklyn. Carolyn and Emily were Barbara's closest friends, and there was also the twins, Gail and Anne Smith. And with the group most of the time was the twins older brother, Charles Smith, and of course his two best friends, Roy Evans, and Sal Gabedian.

Theirs was a very cheerful group of friends. Whenever they got together there was always laughter and vibrant, sometimes heated conversations. Subjects like what they would do for a living when they graduated school, and all kinds of possible future events. These young people actually enjoyed each others company, their bond was strong.

CHAPTER FOUR

Soon after hearing the news of a new brother or sister on the way, Eileen's behavior changed drastically. She began acting out in many different ways, whenever she saw an opportunity, she would cause a commotion, trying to distract whomever from doing whatever it was they were doing, in an effort to regain that attention that has already been lost. The small amount of attention she did get was directed at her hygiene, or lack thereof, and the debate on why Eileen does not do any chores, like every one else.

Once what Eileen called nagging started,, there was no way to stop it. The constant call for her to help out, or at the very least, bathe more than once a week, is the reason Eileen started to leave the house without permission, just up and disappear and never bothered to let anyone know she was leaving or where she was going. Most of the time Eileen would make the journey to Manhattan, and then just wander the streets of New York City with no real purpose in mind, daydreaming about what it would be like to be rich and famous.

It could easily be argued that fate was responsible for introducing Eileen to a woman only known as Kat. At least that's what people that knew her called her. Definitely not her real name, especially when it comes to the kind of work Kat does for a living. An occupation that's illegal, even though its claimed to be the oldest profession in the world.

It was a chance encounter, Eileen usually didn't pay much attention to where she was walking and the way NYC sidewalks are always very crowded, it was only a matter of time before Eileen crashed into another pedestrian, this pedestrian just so happened to be a prostitute named Kat with too much free time on her hands.

When the collision happened, Kats reaction was kind of mean spirited.

"hey little girl, watch where your going!!!" Kat said, and was taken back by the way Eileen mumbled something and just stood there, not making eye contact.

Kat inquired, "hey kid, you in some kind of trouble or something??? You got a name???"

"yea, my name is Eileen, and I'm kind of having trouble at home with my folks"

"Well, if you really want to talk about it, come with me to my place, so we can have a drink and you can tell me all about it. Sound good???" Kat said.

Without much enthusiasm, Eileen agreed to go with this woman to her apartment in Queens, besides, it had to be better than what was waiting for her at home.

The studio apartment was much like what is portrayed on TV and in movies. There were no walls to divide the different living area's. No walls around where the toilet was, just a freestanding, tri-fold privacy curtain.

To Eileen, the strangest thing about the apartment, were the rows of colored beads that partially surrounded the bed. They went from the ceiling, all the way to the floor, with about an inch space between each row. A failed attempt to provide privacy to anyone occupying the queen sized bed.

Kat told Eileen to make herself comfortable and went to the refrigerator, returning with 2 bottles of beer.

So the conversation started with Eileen telling some half truths, and blatant lies. But by the time Eileen started drinking her second beer, all she wanted to do was have Kat tell her all about her life as a prostitute, which Kat was all to happy to do.

After her third beer, it was obvious to Kat that Eileen was a little tipsy. Also, neither one of them were paying attention to the time, and before they knew it, it was already late evening.

So Kat told Eileen, " where exactly do your parents live???, how far is it???"

Eileen answered "we live in Yonkers"

Kat felt that it was too dangerous for a girl her age to have to ride the train through Manhattan at this late hour.

"your going to have to stay here tonight, there's no way I'm letting you take the subway this late, there's a payphone downstairs, I can call your parents if you like, so they know your okay, okay?" Kat said.

Eileen stated that, "no, I can go call them, I seen the phone when we got here, I just need the dime."

So Kat gave her a dime, and off to make her call she went. She didn't even bother to put the dime in the phone, put it in her pocket instead, then picked up the receiver and listened to dial tone for a couple of seconds, just to make it look good in case Kat was watching.

When Eileen returned to Kats apartment, she lied, saying " yea, everything is okay, they said I could stay."

During the ensuing sleepover, Kat turned 2 tricks, and it didn't bother either one of these men in the least, that there was a little girl watching them have sex with this woman.

The next morning, just about the same time Eileen had woke up, there was a knock at the door. Kat sprang out of bed and ran to the door to answer it.

"No I'm not busy, yea I can do that for you before you go to work, c' mon in, there's a friend of mine sleeping on the couch, ok?"

The man at the door replied, "yea, I don't mind being quiet." And handed Kat 50 dollars as he came in and immediately began to undress.

Eileen pretended to be asleep, but through squinted eyes, watched the whole entire interaction. All 6 and a half minutes of it. She was amazed at the sounds they made, Kat was moaning with these high pitched accents, eyes closed, a happy smirk on her face. It was obvious to Eileen that Kat was enjoying herself.

The man on top of Kat was acting a little differently, it almost looked like he was in pain, with this weird kind of grimace look on his face. And unlike Kat, this guy would make a kind of grunting noise every few moments, until finally he let out howl like a coyote, a coyote that smoked a pack a day.

Then they both stopped moving, he climbed off of Kat, gathered up his clothing and went to the sink next to the toilet, gave himself a quick bird bath, got dressed and went out the door and was gone.

Just a couple of minutes later, Kat rose out of the bed, went to the same sink and began giving herself a sponge bath. Eileen took this opportunity to use the toilet, and while she sat there Kat said, " you can use the sink when I'm done, ok, so you can clean up a bit before you go."

"No, that's ok, I can take a shower when I get home, I got to get going, they want me back as soon as possible, thanks for letting me spend the night." Eileen answered as she headed for the door.

"Eileen, you can come visit me anytime you want, my doors is always open for you, ok sweetie?"

"Ok, yea, that sounds great, is the day after tomorrow ok?"

Kat said "anytime you want."

"Ok, by now"

This was definitely a turning point in Eileen's life. She started spending most of her time at Kat's, exposing Eileen to all kinds of detrimental behavior.

Drinking, smoking, swearing, and worst of all, promiscuity, showing Eileen how to use her body to get the things she desires. Eileen pictured herself someday actually becoming a call girl, a high end call girl. She imagined that it would be glamorous and fun. A parade of rich, handsome men for her to entertain, and they would all adore her.

Little did she know, but that particular lifestyle is anything but glamorous and fun.

It was during this time in her life, that Eileen started going through puberty and with that came the new habit of masturbating. She would have wild fantasy's about being with all kinds of different men.

Even though Jack was several years older than Eileen, he had recently picked up the habit of masturbating also.

One night, Jack had unknowingly left his bedroom door ajar while he pleasured himself. Eileen had gotten out of bed to use the bathroom, and heard the strange noises coming from her brothers room. The curiosity was overwhelming, so she decided to investigate. Once she realized what he was doing, she just stood there quietly and watched. She was mesmerized, transfixed, but most of all, enthralled.

To Eileen, her brothers well developed penis was beautiful, even though it was the first one she had ever seen.

"That's why she liked it so much, look at that thing!", Eileen thought to herself.

And just like the men that visited Kat at her apartment, Jack's breathing got heavier, and he let out a moan. Then it happened, with a long kind of growl, he started thrusting his hips, faster, and faster, until with a whisper of a moan, muffled by his pillow, he froze in the upward thrust position and exploded.

Not more than 3 or 4 seconds later, Jack completely relaxed back into his bed, took a couple of deep breaths and fell asleep.

Without hesitation, Eileen retreated to her own bedroom, where as the urge to touch herself was so incredibly enticing, she spends the next 12 minutes doing just that. And for whatever the reason, had a fantasy about what it would be like, if it was her brother doing it to her, just like the men did to Kat.

The events of this particular night, were the very seeds that were planted, beginning an insestual relationship between Eileen and Jack that would last for years.

CHAPTER FIVE

It was just a few months after Eileen met Kat, that the new baby would arrive. Mrs. Barnes gave birth to a baby boy, but unfortunately Larry Barnes was born with a very serious affliction, he was born severely afflicted with Cerebral palsy.

This development would profoundly affect everyone in the family. Everyone except Eileen. She didn't want anything to do with what she called "the little cripple". Eileen would start staying over at Kats, almost every night, only returning home once a week or so, to take a bath and have sex with her brother.

Even though Eileen had made the first move, Jack was all to eager to participate. It was something that they both looked forward to.

But every time she walked in the door, the requests for her to stay and help out with little brother Larry's care began instantly and relentlessly, the whole time she was there. The amount of care he required was enormous, and demanded everyone's help.

But their plea's would go un-answered, Eileen showing her selfish side, only caring about her needs and wants. Oblivious to the hardships the rest of the family was dealing with.

In an effort to try and make the now 11 year old Eileen (she was very tall for her age and looked much older), help out around the house, she was grounded. Forbidden from visiting Kat in Queens.

And on the rare occasion Eileen was allowed to leave the house, it was only with her sister Barbara as a chaperon. The Barnes had most definitely tightened the reins on there daughter Eileen and it was very frustrating for Eileen. This is when she started entertaining the idea of running away. Running away to Atlantic City sounded like a good idea, but she wasn't quite sure how she was going to pull it off.

It was a few weeks before her 12th birthday that Eileen would, on a whim, without any kind of plan and in the spur of the moment, make an attempt to flee.

She would seize an opportunity during one of her parents big arguments. Eileen knew that even though they rarely ever got into a fight, once they did, the disagreement would last for hours, and most of the time, into the next day.

So when the argument began, Eileen quickly gathered up what she thought she would need and crammed it all into a backpack. Then she quietly snuck around the house until she located her mother's purse and stole $100 from it, and immediately left the house.

She was determined to make the journey to Atlantic City and start a new life, away from the dreadfulness that she felt her life was like at home.

During the train ride to Grand Central station, where she needed to transfer to a train bound for New Jersey, Eileen daydreamed about how glamorous and fun her life was going to be, entertaining rich, famous, and powerful men. And all the money she was going to have. Everything was going to be perfect.

Not once did she ever have a premonition of thought about the troubles that lay ahead, starting at the very next stop.

Grand Central station is the perfect title for this transportation hub in the middle of NYC. It's humongous, and a bit confusing. And wouldn't you know it, Eileen ended up getting on the wrong train, heading east towards Kat's, instead of west towards New Jersey. Her next chance to get off the train wouldn't be until Flushing Ave in Queens.

Once she did get off the train, she was unfamiliar with the area she was in, being kind of lost.

Not knowing what to do next, Eileen found a payphone and decided the only choice she had to make it to Atlantic city was to call a cab.

60 dollars and 45 minutes later, she finally made it to Atlantic city. Ad in the 8 dollars that was spent on a burger and fries eaten while waiting for the

cab, left Eileen with less than 15 dollars in her pocket when she stepped out of the cab at 2:45 am.

If she had not been daydreaming about unrealistic, far flung, way out fantasy's the whole trip to Grand Central and been paying attention, so to make the right connection, the trip would have cost her less than 10 bucks.

Good start to a pre-doomed mission.

The first attraction to be visited would be the Boardwalk. She just wandered around without any destination in mind. All the gift shops, and, other assorted stores were closed at this hour, leaving the Boardwalk deserted and empty. An hour later she was standing in front of one of the many Casino's that are the main focus of the area.

With the notion that she had no better idea of what to do with her self, she entered the casino and went straight to a nickel slot machine. With some nickel's that were in her pocket, she started pulling the handle on the machine.

First nickel, nothing.

Second nickel, nothing.

Third time's a charm, the third time she pulled that handle, she hit a jackpot, $80 was the max payout when betting one nickel at a time on that machine. So Eileen cashed out, with a sigh of relief, and decided to move up to the quarter slots. Still betting just one quarter at a time, the machine would pay out a small amount of money, just enough to keep her playing.

For Eileen, winning that first $80, was a lot like when a person decides to take their first hit of crack cocaine. The initial rush feels great, but fades away quickly, leaving the user desperately wanting more.

And that's exactly how Eileen felt, desperately trying to win another jackpot, instantly hooked on gambling, just like a junkie on heroin. She couldn't put those quarters in fast enough, and before she knew it, 12 hours had passed and she was down to just a few quarters. A Nano second later, Eileen put her last quarter in the machine and lost, leaving her completely broke. Her mind went blank, as she sat there staring at the slot machine.

By now it was late afternoon, and Eileen had not one clue as to what she was going to do next. The shadows were stretching out, a sign to Eileen that the day was soon coming to an end. It finally entered her mind that maybe she hadn't thought this plan out, all the way through.

The emotions she felt came and went like a freight train. Discontent was first, believing the situation she was in wasn't her fault. Fear came next, quickly turning to panic when she realized she didn't even have the $7.50 she needed to take the train home.

Just when the panic became to much to bear, Eileen witnessed something. She witnessed a real call girl in action, a seasoned pro at selling flesh. It reminded Eileen about everything she learned from watching Kat sell herself. Heck, Kat made it look easy, Eileen thought to herself, "how hard could it be to get a man to pay me for sex."

Eileen now made the decision to try her hand at prostitution. She felt awkward approaching the different men she saw in the casino, trying to find the right thing's to say. All of her attempts to woo these men failed. It was shocking to most of them that a girl so young would be acting in such a way.

One astonished patron even asked the question, "do your parents know where you are and what your doing?"

What did she expect, her hair was a mess, it was obvious she had no idea what she was doing, and like most kids her age that never shower enough, had a ring of dirt around her neck.

She now became desperate, and started to literally throw herself at these men, jumping in their laps, trying to whisper things in their ear.

Just so happens that the befuddled gentleman's lap Eileen was sitting on, was visiting the casino with his wife, and when this man's wife saw Eileen pawing on her husband like he was a cats toy, she makes a bee line to them.

The wife then grabs Eileen by one arm and bellows, "just what the hell do you think you're doing, you little tramp???"

In a flash, and with her free hand, Eileen hit this woman as hard as she could, causing both of them to fall. The fight was on, the wife was struggling to defend herself. Eileen was fighting like a wild animal, biting and scratching and screaming like a hyena.

Now, if it had been a sanctioned bout with a referee, the woman defending her husbands HONOR, would have been the winner hands down. But it was only with her husband and another patrons help, that they were able to subdue this out of control child.

A moment later, security arrived, taking control of the situation. Ultimately, the Port Authority police department arrived and took Eileen into custody. She was officially charged with Drunk in Public, Assault, Disturbing the peace, and finally, trespassing, being a minor in a casino.

Her parents were contacted and after 5 hours in a holding cell, was loaded into a police van and hand delivered to her parents.

It was 11:35 pm when she snuck out of the house on this mission to escape from the imaginary hardships, just to have the police return her home at exactly 11:22 the next night.

That new, exciting life under the lights, with all its glitz and glamour?

OVER, just 13 minutes shy of 24 hours.

CHAPTER SIX

Mr. Barnes was furious, irate, out of his mind as to what he should do about his out of control daughter. Through much brainstorming and contemplation, he finally came up with a solution.

He would simply call the police and state that his wife and himself could no longer control their daughter, and that she was a danger to herself and others. The police would then have Eileen arrested for being out of control and be held in custody until a foster family became available. Eileen was simply devastated, actually festering hatred towards not just her family, but society as a whole. There was an evil unlike any other growing inside this girl.

The Uncino's were a childless couple with no known relatives.

They lived in a mansion with a total of 8 bedrooms. They bought such a large home in the hope that they would someday fill it with happy children. They longed for, and tried desperately to have children, but were unsuccessful by their own means. The happy couple tried everything available to them at the time. Fertility drugs, physical therapy, they even tried a so called fertility Which doctor, but nothing worked.

And that seemed to be the only thing about their marriage that didn't go right. They excelled in all the other things in their lives, both being very suc-cessful in their respective fields of work.

Mrs. Uncino was an excellent seamstress, producing a line of very popular sun dresses, ultimately selling every single dress she ever made.

Mr. Uncino was a well renowned cartoonist, doing work for the New York Times newspaper and also the New Yorker magazine, winning several awards for his work in the latter.

They would be considered aristocrats, and led a very active social life.

Yes they had fame and notoriety, but what they really wanted never seemed to materialize, to have children, lots of children that could share in the Joy's of their success. They even tried adopting but their always seemed to be some bureaucratic snafu, some legal hurdle that was never overcome.

So when their lawyer suggested being foster parents, the Uncino's quickly agreed and signed up for the program. They were soon notified that a 12 year old girl was available to adopt.

This might be their only chance at raising a kid and even though the child was almost a teenager, they quickly agreed.

Eileen was only in custody for a couple of weeks when she was told a family was interested in her. She could finally get out of jail and be free. She didn't bother to ask or even care what the family was like, all she wanted was to get the heck out of jail, so on her way she went.

Valley Stream is a very affluent bedroom community of NYC that lies between Yonkers and Manhattan. The area is home to the very rich, the very famous, and the most powerful and influential people in New York.

As the car she was riding in started driving by gated community's, and million dollar mansions, Eileen's excitement began to build.

"Were they a rich family?" Eileen wondered.

When the car slowed down and pulled into a driveway with a gate in front of it, Eileen had a grin on her face from ear to ear. She couldn't believe it, what luck, to be adopted by some rich people.

The social worker driving pressed a button on the keypad and a voice was heard through a speaker, to which the worker answered, "yes, social services here to drop off Eileen."

There was a buzzing noise and the gate opened automatically, Eileen was very impressed and couldn't wait to meet her new family.

Eileen was surprised to find that her new parents were much, much older than her original parents. No brothers or sisters??? Eileen was beginning to really like this new living arrangement.

She wasted no time settling in to her new surroundings. And she did a good job of being attentive and engaging, listening to their many success story's, always laughing at their jokes.

"You know, Eileen, you can be a success also, as a matter of fact, you can be anything you want to be. You just have to apply yourself in school." Mr. Barnes said to Eileen one day when she arrived home from school, a private school, no doubt.

"Ok, Mr. Uncino, I know." Was all she said as she hurried off to her room.

Throughout the years Eileen resided with the Uncino's, Mr. Uncino was always trying to motivate his only daughter towards finding an interest in life, something positive and productive. There were no limits as to what Mr. Uncino could provide for an actual future, for Eileen. Mr. Uncino is by all means a somewhat intelligent person. And in line with his strong, well founded beliefs, he was not about to just hand this girl a fortune, she was going to have to earn it.

The requirement was simple, she could attend ANY college she wanted, and major in any subject she desires, and earn a degree in something, prefer-ably something she would enjoy, but at the very least, a degree in something. Then she could have anything else she wanted, a house, a new car, even an expense account.

After spending the better part of an afternoon pleading with Eileen to get an education, Mr. Uncino went so far, as to make it as easy as possible for her, by saying, "sweetheart, even a simple 2 year degree is all I'm asking, ok?, that's it, just 2 years and you can have anything you want."

Later that same evening, as she lay in bed after an hour of fantasizing about money, men, Atlantic city, and gambling, she actually had a glimmer of a thought about her future. There was no way she was going to college for the next two years, not in this life.

She had done as little as possible with her life so far, and wanted to keep it that way. But the constant hounding to make something of herself was making Eileen feel the same despair she felt at her original family's home. So she decided to pretend to be willing to go to college, and let Mr. Uncino pay her tuition.

Not wanting to stray to far from her comfort zone, Eileen chose NYU, right in uptown Manhattan.

And Mr. Uncino finally had hope for his daughters future, unfortunately, it would be a short lived hope.

Eileen did just about everything she was supposed to do, to get started actually attending classes. She met with a guidance counselor, received her complete class schedule, and then wandered the halls of this university that's tucked inside a skyscraper. The classrooms occupied the lower floors, and the dorms took up the top 8 floors, freshmen at the very top, seniors the first floor of the 8.

Eileen never even checked into her dorm room. While she stood in front of the elevator, in the lobby of the dorm, with a blank stare, and an equally blank mind, she couldn't stop dreaming about Casino's, and jackpots. She wanted desperately to go back to Atlantic city.

So instead of getting on the elevator, she tore up her class schedule, along with the other paperwork, tossed it in the air like confetti, turned around and walked out.

She used some of the spending money to get a burger and fries that she ate while contemplating her next move. Out of habit, when she finished eating, she headed to the subway and got on a train heading north, right towards exactly where she didn't want to go, Valley Stream. So she just stayed on the train until it reached the last stop in that direction, Yonkers, right back where she started. And she couldn't wait to see her brother Jack, and get him alone.

CHAPTER SEVEN

When she arrived at the Barnes home, the welcome was anything but warm, and required some pleading from Eileen to gain entry to her former residence. By the next day, Eileen had fallen back into the same old routine, wake up, feed her face, and then disappear, restarting her regular visits to Kats private brothel in Queens.

Eileen also developed a new hobby, harassing her sister, Barbara, for no particular reason.

Eileen would follow her sister every time Barbara went to Brooklyn to visit her friends. Eileen would always find a way to sneak into whatever establishment the friends decided to gather at. Then force her way into hanging out with the group.

Barbara's friends never called Eileen by name, they would always refer to her as "Barb's kid sister"

Eileen didn't really participate in the conversations, she just wanted to be there, and pretend that these people weren't just her sister's friends, but they were her friends as well.

Eileen would always giggle and laugh whenever one of the three boys in the group told a funny story or joke. She considered all 3 of them to be handsome, but was especially attracted to Charles Smith. He seemed to have a way with words, always coming up with the right thing to say to girls, to make them feel good about themselves. All the girls like him.

And most importantly, Eileen's sister, Barbara, more than just liked him, she was in love with Charles Smith. They had recently gone on their first date, and the relationship was going well. From all appearances, it seemed that he had strong feelings for her as well.

A few weeks later, during her normal Saturday Visit to Brooklyn, it happened to be snowing heavily, and for whatever reason, the reunion took place in the basement of an old 12 story brownstone. It was dusty, with just some boxes and a workbench like table, and not much else. It was dry and warmer than outside, and that's all that mattered.

Mere seconds after the group entered the basement, Eileen climbed through the same, narrow, street level window that everyone else used. Knowing her bodily condition, Eileen quickly walked to a box that was off to the side, not to close to the rest of the group. But it didn't help hide her body odor, the smell was overpowering, easily beating out the dust and stale mothballs the room originally smelled like.

It was inevitable that someone in the group would speak up. Someone in the group made the comment, "what the heck is that smell?"

Quick to respond, it would be Charles that said, "that is Barb's runt of a kid sister, she's never heard of soap!"

A couple of "ewe's!" were voiced, and someone told her to go home and take a shower. Barbara told her boyfriend, "apologize to her"

To which Charles answered, "I will not, nobody invited her, you don't even want her around yourself, and you're her sister!"

With that, Eileen slowly walked to the boxes that were stacked under the window and climbed out. Once out on the sidewalk, she started walking towards Queens. After a few blocks, her pace quickened, 2 more, and she started to run, running just about the whole way to Kats place.

With the absurd notion that she was a mother type figure in Eileen's life, a role model of all things, Kat was all ears for her distraught friend, who sobbed through the telling of what happened.

The focus of her anger was because of what was said about her, it was the "runt of a kid sister" comment. That comment stung Eileen like a swarm of bee's, especially coming from Charles. You see, Eileen was in love with him also.

After a couple of Kats beer's, and one of her smokes, Eileen fell fast asleep on the couch, but a storm was brewing on the horizon of what was the next morning, and would soon change her life, forever.

CHAPTER EIGHT

In an attempt to make sure she at least makes it into the Uncino's will, Eileen wrote them a letter, fabricating a wild story about some well to do gentleman that came along and swept her off her feet. Ending the tale with how wealthy this man is and how their engaged and not to worry.

It would be the last time Mr. and Mrs. Uncino ever heard from their one and only child.

It wasn't long before Kat started to realize that Eileen's visits were becoming expensive. Eileen was always bumming smokes, and drinking all the booze, but never brought anything to the table.

Kat was not one to beat around the Bush or hold anything back if she had a problem with something. So Kat made a mention of the fact that cigarettes and alcohol were not free, these things cost money, and that it would be nice if once in a while, Eileen showed up with a six pack in hand or at least her own cigarettes.

Knowing how Kat felt, made Eileen's visits much less frequent. It turned into a kind of bouncing back and forth between home and Kats, splitting her time almost evenly between the two.

Eileen absolutely had no desire to obtain any real life skills, and in her mind, relied on the unlikely fantasy of a life as a prostitute. She believed that she had learned enough about the trade from watching Kat.

The time Eileen spent at home came with requirements. It was 1 of 3 things she must do, to be allowed to stay. It was either go to school, get a job, or help out with poor brother Larry.

The only thing she liked about being at home was the pleasure she got from seducing her brother, which, by the way, was becoming a lot more frequent and neither one of them ever even mentioned anything about some kind of birth control.

It had been a little over 5 years now since Eileen first met Kat and their visits weren't very talkative, like they were the first year these two knew each other.

For the past 4 or 5 weeks, Eileen kept having this nagging feeling, the kind a person has but can't quite understand exactly why, or what. To Eileen, it almost felt like she had missed an appointment or something.

On top of that, during the same time period, she woke up most morning's feeling a little ill, . of sick to her stomach.

She just figured it was some kind of bug, and it would pass.

The very next time Eileen went to Queens to visit Kat, she was surprised to find Kat in an especially good mood, having won $200 on a lotto scratcher.

Kat offered Eileen a beer, but Eileen declined, which was very out of character.

"What's the matter sweetie, are you feeling ok?, you look a little pale." Asked Kat.

Eileen replied, " I'm just a little under the weather, I'll be ok. Can I use the toilet?"

"Of course, sweetie, you don't have to ask "

When Eileen finished going pee, she sat there for a few moments, hoping she would start feeling better soon.

And it was just by chance that she barely glanced at the little waste can next to the toilet just as she started to get up. And whatever it was, made her sit back down for a better look.

When she realized she was looking at a couple of used tampons, she instantly became aware of what was causing that nagging feeling and illness. She realized that she had missed her last two periods. It was the unthinkable, the truly horrifying reality that she was pregnant, pregnant with her brother's baby. The blood instantly drained from her face, and she almost fell off the toilet.

Kat, obviously concerned, went over to the toilet to see how her young friend was doing.

"oh my God!, you look like you need an ambulance!" she exclaimed.

Eileen shot back, "No! Don't call anyone, it's not what you think."

Kat insisted, "come on sweetie, you can talk to me, tell me what's going on."

With a sigh of despair, Eileen finally said, "ok, I'll tell you everything, but first I need a beer and a cigarette!"

So, the rest of the afternoon is spent with Eileen telling Kat everything about how she seen her brother Jack naked and how excited it made her. Also, that once they started, they lost control of themselves and couldn't stop.

"I can't believe I let this happen, what am I going to do?, you're the only other soul in this world that can ever know about this!, I don't want ANYONE to find out about this, not even Jack!"

Once Eileen finally stopped talking, Kat was so surprised by what she just heard, that all she could do was let out a weird noise, like a cross between a sigh and a scream.

Eileen said, "Kat, you got to help me, please, what am I going to do!"

There was now a long uncomfortable silence that lasted for the better part of 20 minutes.

Finally, Kat broke that silence with a question, "does anyone know about you and your brother?"

"No, no one at all. As a matter of fact, everyone I know thinks I'm still a virgin." Eileen said.

There was another few moment's of silence when all the sudden Kats eye's grew wide, and with a devious look on her face, goes on to say to Eileen, "sweetie, I think I got it, actually the solution to your problem is quite simple."

Surprised, Eileen said, "it is?, how so?"

Kat replied, "well, you see honey, you know that guy you like?, the one that was a jerk to you the other day? Charles?"

Eileen asked, "ok, what about him?"

"All you have to do is have sex with him just one time, that's it, just once, seduce him somehow. Maybe even let him think he's getting your virginity. It will work. Then, just wait a couple of weeks, and then go to him and tell him your pregnant, tell him he's the father, there's no way possible it could be anyone else, cause he's the only person you have ever had sex with. That's what you tell him then just watch how everything falls into place. You'll be on your way to everything you ever dreamed of."

If Eileen had been a cartoon character, an animated light bulb would have turned on above her head.

Kat added the advice, "time is of the essence, you need to hurry and have sex with him as soon as possible or the timing will be out of whack."

After another beer, Eileen got up and said to Kat, "I got to go, I have a lot to do to pull this off, wish me luck!"

And off she went, to go find her sister, whom she knew would be visiting her friend's and Eileen wanted to be right there with her.

CHAPTER NINE

To Barbara, her sister was being especially annoying, asking all kinds of questions. Things like when is she going to visit her friends and how Charles was doing and such.

"What do you care about how Charles is doing? You know that I'm going steady with him, right?" Barbara said.

Eileen didn't give an answer right away, and gave a low, halfhearted "yes, I know" as she walked away.

"Just don't you worry about what Charles is doing, you hear me, you little bitch?!" Barbara screamed.

Eileen ignored her sister as she went about planning on how she was going seduce Charles.

So the next Saturday, Eileen didn't tag along with Barbara as she usually did. She stayed far enough behind her sister, so that Barbara thought she didn't have her usual tag along, never getting on the same train, the 10 minute delay, waiting for the next train, was an easy hurdle to overcome.

Once Eileen made it to Brooklyn, it was easy for her to keep an eye on her sister, and stay undetected. After a couple of hours following the group, a panic began to build inside of Eileen's mind, because she had not seen Charles among them.

Then she had a moment of clarity, "since he's not with them, he won't be seeing my sister, and be easier to get him right where I want him." She thought to herself.

After the group had dinner at a pizzeria that sold pie by the slice, the friends said their goodbyes, broke into 3 smaller groups, and parted ways. Roy and Sal headed off in one direction, Barbara, alone, headed for the subway, and Gail and Anne went in yet another direction, most likely homeward bound. And you could bet your last dollar, Eileen was not far behind the Smith twins as they headed home, because that's where here prize was, at the end of that road. For Eileen Barnes, it was just a means to an end.

A half hour later, Eileen was surveying the Smith home from behind a newsstand that was several yards away. The noises that emanated from this neighborhood were mostly the clanging of garbage cans being taken out to the alley behind all these houses.

So Eileen darts off to the alley behind the Smith home, finds their yard, and hides in a shed that is just inside the gate. And waits.

And waits.

Hours pass, until finally, Charles emerges from the back door with two large bags of garbage and hauls them out to the 2 empty cans in the alley. When he comes through the gate, Eileen slides open the door to the shed, revealing herself to him.

With an angry tone, Charles said, "what the hell are you doing here! Are trying to make some kind of trouble!?"

"No! No! Shush! I just wanted see you real bad, I thought there was a spark or something like that between us the last time I saw you guy's." she said with a smile.

"your joking, right? Man, you need to go home, right now." Charles said as he turned to walk away, but Eileen quickly grabbed him by the arm and pulled him towards her, "I just want to ask you something, that's all." Trying to sound soft and sweet.

"Ok, what? What do you want to ask me?" Charles said.

Trying to be as seductive as possible, Eileen said, "actually I have something I want to give you, something special, because I really like you."

"Oh really, you have something for me?, what could you possibly have that I would want?" he said.

"What if I told you it was my virginity that I wanted you to have?" she said as she unbuttoned her blouse, and exposed her breasts, then just as quickly as a moment ago, grabbed his hand and put it on her now exposed breast.

Hormones raging, Charles could barely muster a jumbled response, "Oh!.......really!..........are….you…sure…?"

And with a perfectly timed whisper in Charles ear, Eileen lied to him, and whispered, "this will be our little secret, I promise I won't tell anyone, I swear!"

With that, Charles buried his face in her breast, and Eileen used her foot to slide the door to the shed closed.

That brief moment of lies, passion, and betrayal, would have a stone thrown in a pond effect, rippling through decades of time and dozens of lives.

Eileen followed Kats instructions to the letter, waiting just a little over a week before coming to Charles Smith with this viciously blatant lie. And as luck would have it for Eileen, it happened to be a Saturday that, for whatever reason, Barbara was unable to visit Brooklyn, and totally catch Charles off guard.

Everyone in the group already knew Barb wasn't going to be able to make it to Brooklyn this week, so it was a big shock to Carolyn and Emma when they found their friends kid sister seated at the counter of the local delicatessen.

Carolyn and Emma simply took a seat at a window booth, doing their best not to make eye contact with Eileen.

Didn't matter, no sooner did the two girls sit down, Eileen was already at their table, jabber jawing about nonsense, with the occasional question about Charles thrown in, searching for information.

Emma told Eileen, "you can ask him yourself, if you like, here he comes now."

Charles was alone, disappointing Carolyn and Emma, who both had a thing for each one of his friends. Eileen was glad to see him without his usual companions.

Charles greeted the group with, "what's she doing here?" nodding his head towards Eileen.

"We don't know, I think she's here to see you, hasn't stopped talking about you since she got here."

Charles slid in next to Eileen, grilling her with, "and what exactly do you want with me?"

"Oh, its something kind of personal, I'm really not comfortable talking about it in front of everybody" was her answer.

Carolyn and Emma gave each other these wide eyed, astonished looks, then decided that they were going to the counter and order a fountain drink, giving Eileen the privacy she needed to hook Charles once and for good.

All that the girls at the counter heard was Charles scream, "WHAT, HOW DID THAT HAPPEN!!!"

In almost a whisper, Eileen explained how he was the first, one, and only time in her life she had ever had sex, and he's the only possible person that could be the father.

"Holy crap, what are we going to do?" Charles said.

Eileen answered, "well, WE, are going to have a baby, and I feel you should do the right thing and marry me."

Charles bellowed, "WHAT! ARE YOU OUT OF YOUR MIND!" Then, lowering his voice, " I was thinking more like getting an abortion."

Her answer to that was very clear, "absolutely not, I'm having your baby no matter what, and I don't care who knows about it!"

"But what about "our little secret", huh" he reminded her

"Oh well, that was before you got me pregnant, should have been more careful, besides, I will probably make a better wife than most of these other hussies' running around this block." And that would be all she had to say on that day, rolling her eyes as she got up to leave.

Charles had a panic attack right then and there, and froze like a statue. The girls returned to the booth Charles was still sitting at and tried to find out what just happened.

No matter what they tried, all they got out of Charles Smith that day was, "I don't want to talk about it right now!" and after awhile, Carolyn and Emma left Charles to his own devices.

Besides, it wouldn't be long before everyone they knew, soon found out what happened between Charles and Eileen.

CHAPTER TEN

Eventually, Eileen had to inform her parents about becoming pregnant, and even though she didn't know it at the time, this revelation to her parents would work in her favor.

Eileen's announcement was met with the usual "how's", and "when's", but the most pressing question was the "who" question.

Eileen's mother insisted, "so, I'm going to ask you one more time, young lady, who's the father?"

Eileen didn't have a problem telling her, "Charles Smith."

"What!?, your sisters friend from Brooklyn!? How on Gods green earth……." Eileen's mother went into a tirade as she went to find her husband, so he could do something about it.

Eileen's father's reaction was exactly what she had hoped it would be. He came to her and asked, " do you love him sweetheart?"

"Yes, daddy, I do" was her answer.

"And how old is this boy?" he asked.

"He's 19, daddy" she added.

Her father continues, "well now, that makes him legally an adult, and you still being a minor, I don't see how he has any other choice but to do the right thing, and marry you. As a matter of fact, that's exactly what he is going to do, or I'll have him put in jail for statutory rape."

"Really, daddy?" Eileen squeaked.

Her father said, "You take me to where this boy lives, and we'll settle this matter, right quick!"

Barbara, who was out of town at the time, applying to an out of state culinary arts school, was completely unaware of the events transpiring at home. The news would most likely be devastating, coming out of nowhere, like a UFO in the night sky.

The next day, Eileen and her father would travel to Brooklyn, to meet this boy, and have a talk with his parents.

To Mr. Barnes surprise, Mr. Smith agreed with Mr. Barnes. That, yes it was his son's responsibility to raise this child and that Charles most definitely will do the right thing, and marry Eileen. And not to worry about finances, because his son had recently been accepted into a machinist union.

It looked as though Eileen had pulled it off, turned a possible tragedy, into a triumph, for her it was a means to an end.

So a date was set, and without much say in the matter, Charles Smith was about to enter into a marriage to a woman that he knew he didn't love. But with the pressure on, he had no other choice but to try and make it work.

The marriage license was obtained, and the wedding took place in less than 2 weeks, long before Eileen started showing, which doesn't happen until the 2nd tri-mester of a pregnancy.

The ceremony itself had a strange ambiance, the two families didn't really interact. It was like there was an air of disapproval, not to mention, none of Charles friends attended the wedding.

The only person that was having fun, was Eileen, actually, she was jubilant, her plan had worked out nicely.

So Charles set out to find a living space for his wife and himself, trying to find something within his budget. Not having much luck finding a place in Brooklyn, Charles expanded his search area to include the Bronx and Queens.

Near what's called the garment district, as Charles was on his way to look at another apartment, he noticed a sign in the window of an old 12 story brownstone that read "space for rent, cheap" with a phone number at the bottom.

Charles called the number from a nearby pay phone, and the person renting the space was willing to come over right away, to show Charles the space.

The space for rent was actually the basement under the same building where he found the ad. This basement was unfinished and consisted of the entire space under the building, an immense 3500 sq. ft. It was huge and the price was right so Charles agrees to rent it, as long as he was allowed to make improvements. Even though Charles was a machinist by trade, he was a pretty good carpenter as well. He could see himself turning that basement into a wonderful home.

Eileen, on the other hand was not exactly thrilled about living in a basement. In her minds eye, she was supposed to reside somewhere above the 2nd floor.

CHAPTER ELEVEN

Charles got right to work turning this basement into a home better suited for a growing family. All of his free time was taken up by this project, working on it as soon as he got off work everyday. He made the most progress on the weekends though.

The first thing completed would be the master bedroom, so Eileen wouldn't have to just stare at empty space. Not long after, the kitchen was finished, and all this was done with out any help, and working 50+ hours a week. Eileen not only didn't help out with the renovations, but once the kitchen was done, she avoided it, like an atheist avoids a church.

The weeks and months passed without any real change to this routine. There was the occasional argument over Eileen's responsibility's around the house. She wasn't very consistent when it came to dusting, and laundry.

And she had no desire to learn how to cook, a person actually has to enter the kitchen in order to learn how to use it.

About the only thing Eileen did do consistently, was check the mail, she was eagerly awaiting for the official marriage certificate. And this is when she was able to venture out into world, outside what she called her dungeon, and explore the neighborhood on her way to the post office. The postmaster, for some reason had trouble assigning an address for the basement now occupied by the Smith's. Charles was good at avoiding hassles in life, and simply pur-chased a P.O. box. A couple of months before her first baby was due to arrive, when she checked the mail, she was happy to see that the certificate had finally arrived.

But along with the certificate, was another piece of mail that was addressed to Charles. It had a return address from somewhere in Europe, and the logo of some high profile law firm. She was very interested in, as to exactly what this letter was about.

The most recent addition to Charles renovations was the purchase of a small dining room set that was placed in the corner of the kitchen. So when Eileen returned home from the post office, she went and sat at the kitchen table and opened her marriage certificate. She looked at it over and over again after washing down some kind of barbiturate's with some hot tea that was more cream and sugar, than anything else.

Once her excitement from receiving the certificate had worn off, her thoughts focused on the strange looking letter from Europe. Her curiosity was intensely bugging her mind.

"I am his wife now, and there shouldn't be any secrets between us, so there's no reason why I couldn't read that letter." She thought too herself.

So Eileen opens the letter and begins reading. The legal narrative was very difficult for her to understand and she read this official document over and over again for hours until she finally started to understand exactly what it meant. And when she did, she decided to keep the letter, and the information it contained a secret, for very selfish reasons.

Charles Smith was never given an opportunity to know about the letter, or its contents, information that was intended for his eyes only, for the entirety of his life.

For the now Eileen Smith, it was just a means to an end.

CHAPTER TWELVE

Eileen found Her new life as a housewife extremely dull and boring, and she still made her trips to Queens, which was much closer now that she lived in Brooklyn. And to her despair, her honeymoon was the only other time she had the opportunity to visit Atlantic City and indulge in the only thing she really wanted to do with her life, playing the slots.

Every time Charles got paid from his machinist job, Eileen acted like a dope fiend, bugging him to take her to Atlantic City dozens of times on payday. He was not giving in to her plea's, stating that they couldn't afford it, and what a waste of money it would be.

"WHY NOT!, you get to have everything you want, with all your tools, what about what I want!?" Eileen yelled.

Charles retorted, "first of all, those tools put a roof over our heads, and food on the table!, things you refuse to participate in. I mean hell, you don't cook, you don't clean, you just sit around all day while I'm at work, drinking tea, and reading your story's!"

With that, Eileen flew into a rage, screaming something about not having one of those new electronic gadgets, the television.

Left with nothing else to tell this woman, except that maybe she should take a shower more than once a week, he turned away from her and occupied himself with the ongoing renovations.

The next day, Eileen made her regular, unannounced visit to Queens to visit Kat, and hoped to be able to confide to her older, wiser friend about the imaginary hardships at the hands of her husband.

"He never gives me enough money, he just leaves me to stay home alone all day with nothing to do, its driving me crazy!", Eileen told her friend.

Kats reaction was indifferent, "well, finding a job for yourself wouldn't be a good idea with your baby coming in a few weeks."

Kat knew absolutely nothing about having babies and raising kids, so was unable to warn Eileen about the mountain of chores and responsibility that go hand in hand when rearing children.

That's when Eileen mentioned the letter and how she kept it a secret from her husband. Eileen thought out loud, "there's got to be a way I can get his money from him, as much of it as possible"

In the days that followed, Eileen brooded over how she was going to obtain the assets she learned about from the letter. She spent hours of her time trying to figure out how she was going to steal something that doesn't even belong to the person she must steal it from yet. In other words, she needed to figure out how to steal something from a person that doesn't exist, has not been born yet.

Just days before she gives birth to her first child, she finally thinks she has all the details of her plan worked out, a plan that is the most evil of evil's.

The day she gave birth was the worst day of her life so far, the most pain she had ever felt. She gave birth to a healthy baby girl, a girl she named Eileen Smith jr. to suit her own greedy, selfish needs. A means to an end.

CHAPTER FOURTEEN

With all the drama, and turmoil in his life, Charles didn't talk much to his parents lately.

And there was some turmoil of their very own, separate from the Eileen Barnes debacle. There was a new baby on the way, but it wasn't one of the twins that was expecting, of all people, it was Charles mother, Mae, that ended up pregnant. It was very late in life for the Smiths to be bringing a new life into the world. Mr. Smith was 63 years old at this time, and Mae was a year older, and would be turning 65 a few months before the baby's expected arrival.

There was some genuine concern as to weather Mae would be physically able to carry the fetus to full term. And Mr. Smith's health was already starting to fail, so there was also some concern weather they would be able to physically handle the demands of raising another kid.

So Mr. an Mrs. Smith began to evaluate the immediate family members, trying to figure out who it would be best to ask, to raise this child. Neither one of the twins had any desire to raise their little brother or sister. So the only logical choice was their oldest son, Charles. But since he had just recently became a new father himself, decided to wait at least a couple of months before asking him to take on such a monumental task.

Charles considered himself to have had a good childhood, and loved both of his parents, very deeply. So when it came time for Mae to ask her son for such a huge favor, (Mr. Smith's health had steadily gotten worse in recent months, so much so, he was unable to make the short trip to Queens) Charles didn't hesitate to agree to help, agree to raise this child, as soon as he or she was born.

Eileen, of course, did not take the news well, especially already knowing that Charles wanted at least 2, if not 3 sons. The number of people that would be depending on her to be their mother was growing, and she really didn't want anything to do with motherhood.

In just a matter of months, the size of the Smith family had doubled.

To everyone concerned, it was a big relief when Mae successfully gave birth to a beautiful, healthy baby girl. Even though she knew she would be handing the child over to her only son, Mae wanted to pick the name, and chose Leslie Mae Smith.

After 3 weeks of nursing, Charles, Eileen, and 7 month old Eileen jr. , made the trip to Brooklyn, to pick up the newest member of the family.

With tears in her eyes, Mae handed 1 month old Leslie over to Charles. A discussion then took place about how they were going raise Leslie, or rather, in which context Leslie would be referred to. Would it be Aunt Leslie, or simply Leslie, to give the impression that Eileen Jr. and Leslie were sisters, since they were so close in age. Ultimately, it would be the latter, the fact that Leslie was Charles little sister would be kept a secret, and everyone involved agreed.

Eileen went so far as to conjure up one of her biggest lies, in her life long career of fraud, and it would be told to outsiders, and her future sons, that these girls were paternal sisters, and 3 years separated their birthdays, making Leslie the oldest, even though Eileen Jr was born first.

CHAPTER FIFTEEN

With his childhood missing out on the many benefits of having brothers, Charles was determined to have a lot of sons. He believed in his mind that Eileen got pregnant the very first time they had sex, so having more kids shouldn't be a problem.

It wasn't long before Eileen became pregnant, making Charles excited about the possibility of finally having a son.

Charles had recently finished the girls extra large bedroom, a room they would share. And now he began the task of building what he hoped would be his first son's bedroom. He wanted it to be perfect so it took up most of his attention during the project.

This is when Eileen began a nasty habit of drinking booze, making herself a little bit drunk once a week or so. It would usually be a weekday, while her husband was at work, so to hide this habit from him.

Make no mistake about it, this was not ignorance on Eileen's part, no way. When she was 8 years old, She learned from the neighbors across the street, exactly what alcohol does to a fetus. Eileen had a front row seat when the mother from the childless couple became pregnant. She was already a known lush around the neighborhood, and didn't even seem to slow down. Actually, the last few weeks before she gave birth, she might have stepped it up a notch, carousing around, falling all over the place.

And when the baby came, Eileen noticed that something was off about this kid. As the months passed, it became apparent to most people, that this kid was retarded. The gossip, about how this woman was drunk all through her pregnancy, and was the cause of her baby's brain damage, ran rampant throughout Eileen's neighborhood. It is one of Eileen's most vivid memories from growing up. And now she was going to use that information to her advantage. As Eileen's pregnancy wore on, she became a little more confident, and started getting drunk more than once a week.

Eileen eventually gave birth, exactly a week early, to a somewhat under-weight baby boy. Charles got to pick his sons first name, Theodore, after Charles favorite president, the "rough rider", Theodore Roosevelt. Eileen then demanded that the middle name be Charles, to which, her husband agreed.

Then, as if she had never touched a drop of liquor in her life, Eileen quit drinking, poof, just like that.

This child's life is pre-destined to be rife with troubles.

There were some troubles coming Charles way at the moment, beginning with his wife's behavior towards Ted during the first 12+ months of their son's life.

Other than the basic's, like feeding, and changing diapers, Eileen more or less just ignored the now 18 month old Ted. Had no desire to do any kind of parenting. Heck, "the more retarded, the better" Eileen thought to herself.

Charles was at a loss as to what to do about his lazy wife, so he confided in his best friend, Roy.

"Man, I don't know what to do about this worthless bitch", Charles complained.

He continued with, "she's not teaching him anything, she wouldn't even teach him how to tie his shoes!"

"Well, about the best you can do now is wait till he's old enough, and take the boy to work with you." Roy advised his friend.

Charles added, "you know, your probably right, that's a real good idea, I think that's exactly what I'll do."

Charles's daughters would soon be old enough to pick up the slack left behind by Eileen's complete lack of interest in being a housewife.

And Eileen would soon become pregnant again, and just like her last pregnancy with Ted, she picked up her habit of getting drunk once or twice a week. But with the renovations almost complete, it was becoming harder to get away with her once a week drinking binges and towards the end of the pregnancy, Charles was able to put a stop to her drinking, altogether.

CHAPTER SIXTEEN

Something else happened during this pregnancy that would bring about a major change to the Smith's living situation.

One night during this time, while everyone was sleeping soundly, Leslie was awakened by some strange noises coming from the living room, it sounded like someone was moving around the apartment in the dark, bumping into things. She also thought she heard someone whispering to someone else.

She climbed out of bed and quietly went to see what was causing all the commotion. When she reached the hallway that led to the living room, she saw two men wearing ski mask's, moving around that part of the apartment, rummaging thru all their stuff. Unable to find anything of real value to steal, the crooks snatched up the Smith's brand new TV, and climbed out the same street level window they had entered through. Leslie, still frozen with fear, and not knowing what she should do, simply went back to her room and fell asleep.

The next morning, Charles was irate, very upset that someone broke in just to steal their new TV.

But when Leslie told everyone what she was witness to, would cause Eileen to become very upset as well.

"What if they decided to hurt one of us, or hurt one of the kids?!" would be one of her many concerns.

This incident was part of the changes going on in society at the time, early in 1970. The free love attitude of the hippie movement was at its height, and drug use was becoming widespread, spreading like a grass fire through the younger generations. And that drug culture brought with it a mess of other problems. Mostly crime, property crimes skyrocketed, and the bigger cities around the country were becoming increasingly more dangerous, especially New York.

Even Charles had to admit that the city was becoming too dangerous of a place to raise his growing family.

With a heavy heart, Charles started looking for somewhere far away from the madness of the city, to move his family to. And Charles wanted to make sure that the move happened well before the arrival of newest family member.

The estimated due date for their baby was the first week of June. It was almost Valentine's day, so it gave Charles a good 3 months to find a safer place to live. He was having trouble finding an existing home that suited his needs, and would start exploring how much it would cost to have one built.

Charles was never comfortable conducting any kind of business over the phone, so its no surprise that Charles would shop the different home builders in person.

While visiting one builder in particular, he noticed a home that was very close to completion with a for sale sign out in front of it. When Charles had found the jobsite superintendent, he inquired about this un-finished home.

The super stated, "Oh, yea, that house? The buyer backed out of the contract at the last minute, and its available. You can check it out if your interested."

The house was a 3 bedroom, with a storm cellar that was basically a basement the same size as the space above it, minus a single car garage that had a sloping driveway. Good sized yard as well.

To Charles, it was perfect, and asked the super who he would talk to about buying the home.

The super gladly put Charles in contact with the agent selling these homes, and the details were worked out, and a contract was signed with a lender.

Charles just purchased a home, a major milestone in his life. With a considerable amount of work to be done before the Smith family could move in, the builder informed Charles that the turnover date would be Friday, May 8th 1970. It was perfect, a whole month before the new baby was due.

CHAPTER SEVENTEEN

Eileen and her daughters were very excited about moving into a brand new home, and chatted constantly about all the benefits and amenity's that come with home ownership.

Eileen really wanted to show off HER new house to as many people as possible after they finally got to move in, in early May. One day Eileen realized that the date they get the keys to their new house was a couple of days before Mothers Day. She got to thinking that it would be a lot of fun, AND a really great way to show off her new house, if she could have a Mothers Day house warming party for herself, and invite some friends and family.

She was not very optimistic about asking her husband if she could have this party at their new house on Mothers Day, and was very surprised when Charles really liked her idea, and gave her a green light for her party.

He hoped that letting her plan the party, and have the responsibility of getting everything ready, she would be more motivated to actually do some housework, and help maintain their new home.

So plans were made, party supplies were purchased, and invitations sent out. All with the help of her 2 daughters, Leslie and Eileen Jr. These girls were almost as excited as their mother about this party, they could hardly wait.

As luck would have it for the whole family, the builder was able to give the keys to their house, to them, a day earlier than scheduled. This gave everyone an extra day to get moved and settled in, before this big party they were going to have.

Although Charles was able to put a stop to Eileen's drinking of late, she felt she had not achieved her goal in manipulating this next child's future.

So the Saturday night before the party, Eileen decided to sneak herself a pint of gin. She hid the bottle between her legs, under her moo moo, as she sat at the same small kitchen table she sat at in Queens.

Charles was busy doing stuff in his new basement, and didn't know anything about the bottle of gin.

Around 1:15 in the morning, Charles had finished whatever he was doing and came upstairs to get ready for bed. As he passed Eileen, he said, "you coming to bed, or what?"

"As soon as I finish this article I'm reading." Was her answer, she needed a few more minutes to polish off the bottle of gin. After which, she decided to actually read some article about some hero, mostly so she could enjoy her buzz.

It was about 1:45 am when Eileen got up and stumbled towards the hallway, on her way to bed. When she reached the hall bathroom, she felt the slightest twinge between her legs, and hoped she just had to pee. When she sat on the toilet, she actually did go pee, and after she finished wiping, she felt an all to familiar pain in her groin.

"Please, not now, please!" she mumbled to herself.

It was a contraction, and she simply ignored it and headed to bed. Right as she was climbing into the bed, her water broke, followed by another, more intense contraction. Then she let out a very loud moan, waking her husband.

"What's the matter?", he asked.

Sounding irritated, "my water just broke, I think we should go to the hospital, I'm pretty sure the baby is coming."

With a depressed sigh, Charles said, "ok, go wait in the car, and I'll get your suitcase ready, then we'll go."

When they arrived at the hospital, Eileen realized that she was still a little drunk. She hoped nobody noticed. She also realized that this would cancel her big party.

She thought to herself, "this little bastard wasn't supposed to be here until next month, this little fucker ruined everything!"

Her contractions were now less than 5 minutes apart, almost time.

A couple of hours later, Eileen gave birth to a baby boy.

William Charles Smith was born at exactly 5:48 am on Sunday May 10th , Mothers Day. He was 4 weeks premature, born drunk, and actually hated by his own mother, before he even took his first breath of air.

And the coldest part of Eileen's game? Those two pregnancy's were the ONLY times in her life she ever used alcohol.

A MEANS TO AN END.

CHAPTER EIGHTEEN

Even before the dust had settled from the move and canceled party, Eileen went about creating a façade for her new neighbors to see, she wanted to paint a picture for them. She wanted the neighbors to believe that Charles was abusive to not just the kids, but her as well.

Eileen wanted the neighbors to see her husband like he was some kind of monster. But the only time he ever even came close to acting like a monster, is when something or someone was trying to hurt his family or himself.

Although Charles did spank his children a few times, he was actually very good at finding creative, non-violent ways to punish his kids.

On one occasion, Charles decided to punish Leslie for failing to do her homework on a regular basis right after school.

So instead of a spanking, the man decided to take away Leslie's phone privileges for the next 2 weeks. He felt that she spent way too much time on the phone after school, and was likely the reason she couldn't complete her school assignments on time.

So when Leslie was caught by her father using the phone before the 2 week sentence was up, she still didn't get spanked, instead, Charles simply walked over to the phone, and pressed the receiver button ending the call.

Leslie then went berserk, attacking her father viscously, leaving him with scratches on his face and neck.

Knowing the neighbors most likely heard the commotion, Eileen saw this as another opportunity to smut up her husband, telling her neighbor next door,

" he just walked thru the door and started beating Leslie, just because she was using the phone!"

She continued, making it sound like he was so cruel to everyone, that the kids were forbidden to even use the phone.

Eileen had these people baited, hook, line, and sinker. And the neighbors didn't bother to look for evidence to back these claims up.

Around this time, Eileen became pregnant once again, but this pregnancy would be very, very different from the others. For starters, there would be no more once a week poisonings for this fetus, she needed this child to be normal, without defects of any kind. She even quit smoking cigarettes for the duration of this pregnancy.

Charles Brian Smith was born sober, without the same birth defects that were inflicted on his older brothers. Eileen made sure this child was healthy, and did so by design, on purpose, to suit her own needs. She also paid a lot more attention to this child, and for a very brief span of her life, she made a half hearted attempt at actually being a parent to one of her children. She finally did things like teaching Brian (since Charles middle name is Edward, the younger Charles was not a "Jr", or, "the second", and thus was always referred to by his middle name) his A,B,C's, and how to tie his shoes, and brush his teeth, the latter being something Eileen didn't do on a regular basis, herself.

Another one of the biggest lies Eileen Smith has ever told, is the web of deception she created, concerning her children's actual age and year born. The real timeline for the year each one of them was born puts Eileen Jr in early '66, Leslie in late '66, Theodore, June '68, William, May '69, and finally, Brian, July '70.

But as far as any one of the Smith sibling's knew, the year that they were told, that they were born, was much different.

Eileen found a way to forge each child's birth certificate, changing only the year each one of them was born. That's all she needed to change.

So now it put Leslie first to be born in '65, then, Eileen Jr, in early '67, Theodore, June '67, William, May '70, and Brian, July '73.

She wanted distance between these brother's and sister's, so that they would always have different interest's growing up, therefore, never spending any time together, destroying any kind of bond or comradery amongst these sibling's, long before one ever had a chance at forming.

CHAPTER NINETEEN

Most of Williams memories begin around the time he turned 4 years old. He had very fond memories of his childhood years in New York, especially the snowfall that always returned in the winter, most definitely his favorite season of them all.

When it snowed, the number of activity's for kids, teenager's, and adult's, double's, maybe even triples.

A wealth of fun things to do are now available, games, and competitions of many sorts.

Williams favorite snow time activity was making snow angels. Every time the back yard canvas was wiped clean with fresh snow, William couldn't wait to go outside and start making them. And not just 1 or 2, he would make 15 or 20 of them at a time, spending hours at a time doing it, and using the entire back yard.

Then he would climb up a couple of steps on the back stoop, and marvel at his personal army of angels, and that they were there to watch out for him. Unlike the way most of the rest of the family simply ignored William. No nurturing from his mother, no friendly advice from his siblings, causing William to be very naïve in character.

For some reason, right before William started the 1st grade, he started wetting the bed, almost every night. He would basically get away with it during the week, when his father was at work. But on Saturday's and Sunday's when

Charles didn't have to go to work, it was impossible for William to hide his bedwetting from his father.

It was not a pretty picture. Charles, being the bread winner, cook, and disciplinarian, was obviously spread very thin and very stressed. That might be the reason the first couple of times Charles discovered his son wet the bed, William was dealt, bare ass, leather belt spanking's that took place in the living room, for all to see.

The third time this happened, as William went crying to his room, Eileen Jr and Ted were laughing, and ridiculing their brother, which only amplified his already meek demeanor.

When Charles seen this belittling, he literally broke down, right then and there.

He slumped back into his arm chair and tears of his own, filled his eyes, and he thought to himself, "what am I doing!, this is not how this is supposed to go!, something's got to change!"

Charles then retreated to his favorite part of the house, the basement, where he would use his tools to occupy his hands, so he could clear his mind and figure out a better solution.

It was almost Thanksgiving, and the next time William wet the bed, his heart almost beat out of his chest, because of the fear he felt when he noticed his dads car still in the driveway. It was a school day, which meant he just might get the belt, right before school.

William hurried to the bathroom for a quick shower, then got dressed. No sign of his dad so far. Then to the kitchen, where there might be, or might NOT be some kind of breakfast. It was nearing the time for the school bus to arrive, so as fast as he could, slapped some jelly on some slices of bread and headed out the door. Williams heart was racing, but to his surprise, he still hadn't seen his father and felt a little relief as he stood with some other kids at the bus stop, that was a few houses down the street from his.

"I think I made it." William thought to himself as he waited, confident he got passed his father, undetected.

When the school bus came into view, William started to feel good about the start to this day.

But as the bus pulled up to the curb, the kids already on the bus exploded in a chorus of giggles and laughter. William thought maybe one of the other kids was getting cut up on. When William turned down the isle of the bus to take his seat, he would see the front of his house for the first time that day, and now knew exactly what all the other kids were laughing at.

There, for the whole bus to see, was Williams pissy sheet, hanging out of his bedroom window. He was the reason for their laughter. He did his best to not make eye contact with the other kids as he sat down. He was so embarrassed, he spoke not one word to ANYONE, not even his teacher, the whole rest of the day.

Some people might view this as cruel and unusual punishment, but this incident is when it all came to an end.

And some people might ask, "why?"

That answer to that question is quite simple, the man didn't want to spank his kid any more. Period.

The bedwetting and beatings? DONE! OVER!

Charles never, EVER, spanked his son, ever again.

And William, from that very day, to this, never, ever, wet the bed again. Later in life, William would come to really appreciate what his father did for him that day.

CHAPTER TWENTY

In 1975, Christmas day was a Saturday, which made Christmas eve Friday night.

In New York city, Anyone with a pulse was going to, or doing some, serious partying.

The Smith house is referred to as what's called a "row house", because of the way their in a single row and they all have the same basic floorplan. This put the living room at the front left corner of the home and all 32 homes had a large picture window that faced the street.

And everyone on the block, put their Christmas tree in that picture window. Over the years, it became a kind of unofficial contest among the resident's, as to who had the nicest tree.

The company that Charles worked for, hosted a Christmas eve party for all of its employees, which, with his wife, he was going to attend.

This left Leslie and Eileen Jr, who were almost teenagers, to babysit their 3 younger brothers. As soon as their parents pulled out of the driveway, the 3 older Smith children, started a party of their own they had planned when they found out they would be left alone at home that night.

Eileen Jr had gotten her mother to provide her a fifth of Everclear, that they didn't even come close to finishing. The Smith's told their children they would be home by 1:00 am. By 11:30 pm, the trio were completely drunk, running around laughing and screaming like out of control soccer fans. All the commotion scared the heck out of William, he pleaded with them to stop, but they paid absolutely no attention to their brother, and William buried his head under his pillow, hoping his parents didn't come home early.

They didn't, actually they were almost an hour later than they said they would return.

And it didn't make a difference anyway, because the damage had already been done, and the 3 party animals were all passed out before midnight.

As soon as Charles pulled in the driveway, he instantly knew he was going to cancel Christmas this year. There was trash all over the front yard and someone had knocked over the tree, and it was sticking out the broken picture window. When he went inside, he found his three oldest, passed out in different locations around the house. A half full bottle of Everclear was found in the kitchen.

Charles decided to leave all 3 right where they lay, tucked the bottle of booze under his arm, dragged the Christmas tree out back to his burn barrel and used the booze to light that tree on fire. Then he just stood there quietly and watched it burn until it was completely gone.

The next morning Charles woke up long before his 3 little home wreckers, and immediately began making trips to the family wagon, filling it with all the gifts that had been purchased in the weeks prior. All of them, including gifts he bought for his wife and himself. He spent the better part of the next week returning those gifts to the different stores where they were bought.

When Charles finished loading the wagon, he found that William was the only one of his children that was awake, sitting in the Christmas tree-less, living room, deflated look on his face.

Charles told William, "c'mere, I want to smell your breath.", then, " breathe in my face.", and finally, "good man, you have anything to eat yet?"

"No." was Williams simple, to the point answer.

"c'mon, I got a couple of things I want you to help me out with today, ok?" Charles told him.

"Ok, dad", William replied with a smile.

After some oatmeal, Charles said, "follow me", and William followed his dad, to his own bedroom closet, where the attic entrance is located.

The gun cabinet was always kept locked and in the attic, and after some instruction on how to properly handle a weapon, William helped his father carry all the guns he owned to the living room couch, one by one.

"Are we going hunting today, dad?" William inquired.

"No, son, this year for Christmas, I am going to give you the gift of responsibility.", and Charles proceeded to patiently teach William, by letting William preform all the task's, himself, how to properly handle, dismantle, clean, and reassemble the 12 gauge Remington 8 shot shotgun.

Then, had William do it again, without the prior guidance, and was confident that his son could properly handle the weapon, treat the gun with respect. Charles went to the basement and returned with a box of shells, telling William, "c'mon boy, lets have some fun!"

William followed his dad to the back yard, that had an extended forest right behind it. Charles then taught his son how to load the shotgun, engage a round, dis-engage that round, and completely unload the weapon.

Charles then told his son to load the gun and chamber a round, "now, put your left hand on the pump, grab the trigger handle with your other hand and put your finger on the trigger guard, like I showed you." Charles instructed him.

Charles continues, "bring the but up to your right shoulder, and point it out into the woods. Now use your right eye to look down the barrel to aim at what you want to hit. Ok. You got it?"

William nodded his head to confirm that he was ready.

Then Charles whispered to his son, "now put your finger on the trigger and pull"

#! BAM !#!!!!

The recoil almost knocked William on his ass, but being tall for his age, he was able to weather it.

As William was rubbing his shoulder, his dad asked him,

"Did that hurt?"

"Yea a little, kind of like when Ted punches me in the arm."

Charles said, "you want to fire off a few more rounds,?"

William quickly answered, "yea, ok, I do."

"Ok, listen here, I am going into the house, and when I say now, fire a round into the woods, then chamber the next round right away, then wait for me to say now again, and fire another one, every time I say now, you fire that gun, ok?"

"Ok, dad, I will!" William said excitedly.

Charles stood over a still passed out Eileen Jr and loudly said "NOW"

#! BAM !#

He heard William chamber the next round, as Eileen Jr stirred around a bit for a couple seconds.

"NOW"

#! BAM !#

Eileen Jr now started tossing and turning and mumbled something.

"NOW"

#! BAM !#

The third time William fired that shotgun, Eileen Jr sat right up, with a gasp, looking her father right in in the eye, and Charles, in a low, angry voice, said, "now, if you and your bonehead partners in crime don't want to end up in foster care, I suggest you three idiots have this mess cleaned up before me and your little brother get back from lunch, I'm taking him to Nathan's in the city, to reward him for having more sense than the three of you jackasses put together."

CHAPTER TWENTYONE

Ever since Charles got his son to stop wetting the bed, their relationship changed noticeably. William would now go places with his father a lot more often. Charles had gained a certain amount of respect for his soon to be seven year old son, unlike his first son, Ted, who acted very unruly at times, and would sometimes decide to ignore his father, altogether.

The respect Charles now had for William, stems from the fact that William was able to conquer the bed wetting demon quickly, giving Charles hope that his kid had a good head on his shoulders.

During this time in his life, William was becoming ever more separated socially, from all the rest of the family, besides his dad. The older 3 siblings called him a "brown noser" or a "kiss-ass", because of the way Charles favored William. What did they expect, William was the ONLY one of 5 family members that actually listened to what the man of the house said. Add in the very ugly animosity the three women of the house have held on to ever since the cancelled party, way back when William was born, its no surprise that William never felt accepted by these "people". Even had this un-safe feeling from time to time.

One of Williams memories that sticks out in his mind, is how one Saturday morning in the fall of '76, Eileen was "allowed" to go and do the weekly grocery shopping. This was a rare event, Eileen didn't have a drivers license, and meant that Charles was just too tired to go himself.

Charles was well aware that William always tried his best to always be on his best behavior, knowing as long as he didn't get into any trouble, like his sisters and brother did on a weekly basis, that he would always get to go with his dad whenever Charles left the house to run errands, or buy stuff they had run out of.

Not wanting to deny William his weekly excursion, and disappointing Eileen, Charles insisted that Eileen take William with her to do the shopping.

"the kids good help, smart too." Charles praised his son.

Most of the trip was uneventful, but what stuck out in Williams mind, is how on their way back with the groceries, Eileen pulled into the parking lot of a local fast food restaurant, and went inside. Out of habit, William went inside with her. Eileen didn't notice her son was with her, until right before she placed her order.

She snapped, "William! Go wait in the car!"

"its okay mom, dad NEVER makes me wait in the car, he says "you never know when or where you might learn something." William informed his mother.

She placed her order, then went and sat down with a double cheese burger that came with a large order of fries. She also had two drinks on the tray, iced tea for her and a water for William.

As he watched his mother eat her burger, she said something to William that he never forgot.

"I'm sorry, honey, it will be ok, you can have something to eat when we get home, ok?"

She continued, "he never gives me enough money, that son of a bitch!"

After the last bite of burger, "I'll get his money, you watch, all of it!"

As they left the restaurant, she threw the untouched order of fries in the trash, as if she was all alone, and no one else in the world might be hungry.

Charles rarely went out on a Sunday, but the very next day, William was treated to another excursion with his father. The two drove to a Sears department store in Queens. Charles went straight to the appliances, and looked around a bit until Charles saw exactly what he was looking for. Him and his son were now standing in front of a portable dishwasher, the kind that hooks up to the kitchen faucet, a nice one, even had a hardwood cutting board top.

A sales agent approached the father and son, but before he could say much, Charles cut him off with, "I'll take it."

The idea behind the new appliance, was to try and motivate his wife to do something, ANYTHING, around the house. A new appliance can sometimes accomplish this. Unfortunately for everyone in the house, they used it way more than she did.

William remembers an incident that happened one night right before he turned 7.

Just as everyone sat down for dinner, a fight started between Charles and his wife. Screaming fits would be a better description, Eileen always yelling at her husband about not having this, and not having that. Her biggest gripe was how she didn't have a car to drive, like all the other wives on the block.

His stance on the issue was always the same.

"Woman, I told you a dozen times, go to the DMV, get yourself a license to drive a car, and I'll get you something nice to drive." He told her.

Upon hearing this, Eileen flew into a rage, screaming obscenity's, and smashing dishes on the floor.

As he pleaded with her to stop, he slammed his fist on the table, catching the edge of his plate, sending pasta an sauce all over the walls and ceiling.

Weather it was to get away from her abuse or some other reason, Charles retreated to the basement.

Eileen paced back and forth, wanting to yell at her husband some more.

A few minutes had passed, when Charles decided to come back up stairs. When Eileen heard him start climbing up the stairs, she ran over to the dishwasher, unhooked it from the sink and rolled it to the top of the staircase and waited.

When Charles came around the corner of the L shaped staircase, Eileen shoved that appliance down the stairs at him. But instead of letting that dishwasher smash into him, he caught that thing like someone would catch an oversized beach ball, literally wrapping his whole body around this 125 lb. chunk of metal, plastic, and wood, and rolled all the way back down the stairs to the basement. And that's exactly where Charles and HIS appliance stayed the rest of the night.

He didn't even come upstairs before leaving for work the next day. And that appliance? Well it stayed in that basement for the next 45 years, becoming a permanent part of the basement, after Charles eventually turned that part of the house into a separate dwelling, by removing that upper part of the stairway and replacing it with a landing and an exterior door. Obviously an attempt to erase the events of this night, from his memory. To this very day, that appliance is still right there where he installed it, and does not have one scratch on it.

CHAPTER TWENTYTWO

William would be turning 7 years old very soon, and last year was the first year Williams remembers ever celebrating the event. And it was true, his 6th birthday was the first one that was ever celebrated by his family. The first 5 of these milestones in Williams life were just ignored, nah, didn't matter to any of these "people", it was even said by one of the 3 women in the house, that, "Williams birthday?, so what, who gives a shit."

What did it matter to William anyway, why should he miss out on something, that should have been done for him, but wasn't.

And when this years birthday arrived, their was some kind of big argument, and the event went back to being ignored.

It really didn't bother him that much, and in later years, got used to not celebrating it.

But what was bothering William at the time was this big trip that his mother had planned for the next week

The thing that bothered him the most was that his dad was the only person in the family not going on this trip. And this trip was to California, of all places, and by bus, no less.

Eileen would insist on going to California for 3 weeks, to visit her parents, whom had relocated to a large farming community, in central California's, San Joaquin Valley.

Eileen knew good and well, that there would no way her husband would be able to take a whole month off of work.

The labors of a high end machinist, are tedious and demanding, both physically and mentally. Schedules and deadlines are strict as well.

Even two weeks would be out of the question, and one, definitely a hard sell.

Did Eileen really want Charles to be with her in California? NOT. She didn't want him to know what she was really doing there. She claimed it was so that her parents could see all their grandkids at once, maybe for the last time, her parents being on, in years. But this was only partially true.

This made it viable in Charles mind, and he agreed to fund this trip across the whole country, which, by no means, was cheap. As a matter of fact, it cost a small fortune.

In Williams minds eye, he was confused, he didn't understand why she was taking all of them to California. To William, 5 kids on a bus, for 5 days, seemed like an awful lot of trouble to go through, Just to visit a bunch of people, she didn't even like in the first place.

Schedules were checked, tickets were bought, bags were packed, and off to California they went. William had mixed feeling's about this adventure he was embarking on with his family. It had an air of excitement to it, being his first time outside New York City. The sights were truly amazing, like how hugely wide the mighty Mississippi River is, or the St. Louis Arch. Even got to see Mount Rushmore.

William was also treated to one of the strangest, somewhat amazing, visualizations a person might ever see. It was during the middle part of the trip, while traveling across the Great Plain's of The United States. This part of the country is EXTREMELY flat, less than a 1% grade from the Mississippi river, all the way to the foot of The Rocky Mountains.

William was sitting at the front of the bus, while the rest of his family took seats at the back, drinking and carrying on with the other passengers. William was politely trying to make conversation with the driver. 20 questions was more like what it really was, this Bus Company employee, going above and beyond the call of duty, not just putting up with the shenanigan's from the back seats, and keeping them all safe, but doing his best to entertain this little boy suffering from cabin fever.

"What's your name, son?" the driver asked.

"William."

The driver then said, "Ok, William, you want to see something pretty neat?"

"Yea, ok."

The driver went on to tell William, "you see that little dot, out on the horizon?"

William, "yea, I see it."

The driver now instructed William, "ok now, you just keep your eyes on that little speck, don't look away from it, just keep staring at it, ok?"

"ok, Mr., I will." And began to watch this little dot. And with a straight, flat, empty road in front of him, the driver pushed a little harder on the gas pedal, so to amplify this visual effect.

"You see anything yet?" the driver asked William.

William replied, "kind 'a, whatever it is, its getting bigger."

"What's it look like now?" after a couple of more minutes.

"it keeps getting bigger, like its growing right before my eyes!" William answered.

"what do you think it is?", the driver asked.

"I don't know, WHAT do you think it is?" William shot back.

William was watching the next city down the road, literally growing right before his eyes, like watching a plant grow using time lapse photography. And before you knew it, there it was, in all its glory, Kansas City.

"wow, that was pretty neat, thanks". And then just sat quietly, waiting for the next opportunity to watch the next city down the road, grow right out of the ground.

Williams strongest feeling about this trip is that he wished his dad was right there with them, "wish dad was here to see this", would be the dominant thought in his mind throughout the trip.

California really didn't impress William all that much. The first thing he noticed when he got off the bus was the extreme heat. The temperature topped out at 101° degree's that day, and it was still May. Also, The place was way to bright, and everybody was wearing sunglasses. For the most part, the actual visit was boring and uneventful.

But something truly profound would happen to William during his visit to California, and would affect William, in many ways, and for many years.

Eileen's parents two bedroom apartment didn't even come close to accommodating Eileen and the kids. And even though Charles had given her enough money for all the possible expense's, Eileen chose to stay over at an old acquaintance's house.

This friend of Eileen's had two sons of her own, Keith and Chad. They were much, much older than the Smith children, with Chad, the younger of the two, being 9 years older than William. The sleeping arrangements, put William in Chad's room for their stay. The age difference was a factor between the two, and they had really nothing at all in common.

The second night of his stay in Chad's room, something happened. Chad did something to William that he had absolutely no right to do.

As William slept quietly on a mat on Chad's floor, about 12:30 am, Chad quietly got out of his bed, and lay right next to William. Chad then gently pulled back the blanket William was under, and without a warning or anything of that sort, Chad put his hand down Williams underwear and started fondling Williams penis. A few moments later, William woke up with a hard-on and Chad was stroking it. Before William could have any kind of reaction, BAM!, it happened, William had his very first orgasm. It was so powerful, that he actually seen stars.

Fear, confusion, excitement, William didn't know what to feel. One thing he knew for sure was that it felt good, really good.

As Chad climbed back in bed, William asked, "what did you just do to me?"

Chad whispered, "I made you cum."

And that's all that was said between the two of them that night. It took a little while for Williams heart to stop beating so fast, and even longer to fall asleep. He couldn't stop thinking about what just happened to him. That night dominated his thoughts so much, that he doesn't even remember the trip to Yosemite, and the bus ride home was just a blur. For months after they got home, he would think about that night.

The money Charles gave his wife to stay in a hotel for their visit and keep her children safe was spent on something else, it was spent at the local bingo hall. BINGO!

But soon, mother nature would get William to forget all about that night, and California itself, for that matter.

CHAPTER TWENTYTHREE

September, right in the middle of hurricane season. On or about September 15th, 1977, hurricane Bill, (irony at its best) came off the coast of Africa, just like every other storm before it. But when "Bill" reached the Caribbean, it took a hard right turn, staying out over the Atlantic as it moved north, not making landfall until it reached New York. Very rarely does a storm of this magnitude (category 2, 115 mph sustained winds) ever strike New York City, not even once in a hundred years. But this one did, made a direct hit on New York City.

For William, this had to be in the top 5 most scariest moments of his life. Heck, "moment" is a HUGE understatement. This ordeal was 16 hours of straight madness. There were mandatory evacuations for everyone within a mile of the beach.

The Smith family, as well as the rest of the block, were going to stay put, ride out the hurricane in their storm cellars.

As Charles was making preparations, securing storm shutters and bringing their pets inside, he told his son Ted, who was still in his bedroom, "get your ass in the cellar!"

Ted defiantly told his dad, "I'm not hiding from some stupid storm in the cellar with the rest of you sissy's!"

Charles's oldest son was going thru the "I'm 12, and I know everything" phase of growing up, and he was having a hard time getting his son to listen to him and obey his wishes.

Everyone else in the family, already in the basement, were expecting Charles to bring Ted to the basement by force. But that didn't happen, what did happen was another example of Charles using non-abusive, creative ways to discipline the children he genuinely cares for.

So the conversation between father and son ended with Charles, "fine, have it your way." And he went on to finish what he was doing and then made his way to the cellar.

When he sat in his recliner, he let out an exasperated sigh, and said, "if this storm don't knock some sense into that kid, nothing in this whole world ever will."

About an hour later, the wind started blowing really hard, making a wicked sound, like a group of people screaming at the top of their lungs, with high pitched screeching every few moments. The sound gave the impression that the wind had always been blowing, and was never going to stop. It got so loud, every one covered their heads.

The sounds of glass shattering, and tree trunks snapping could be heard coming from outside. The house shook violently, popping, and creaking, making all kinds of noise. William wondered how his brother was fairing upstairs.

What happened next, was nothing short of a miracle, disguised as a tragedy.

A very thick, very tall pine tree that was right across the street from the Smith home, succumbed to the brutality of the hurricane, and fell. Making a direct hit on Theodore's bedroom.

And the miracle of all this, is that Ted had not one scratch on him, as a matter of fact, he must have been more scared than he led on, because that kid was in the basement and under the covers, before that tree stopped rocking back and forth, just a couple of feet above Williams head.

It was the only time in Williams life, that he ever heard his father laugh.

But the thing that left William awestruck the most, about the whole ordeal, is that, the next day, when he was allowed to venture outside to survey the damage and destruction, the first thing he noticed was that EVERY SINGLE BLADE OF GRASS, had been stripped off the lawn. All that was left, was bare dirt, and even it looked traumatized.

CHAPTER TWENTYFOUR

For the next several years, things didn't change much around the Smith home. Eileen still refused to even try and pretend to be a housewife. William started to notice his mother didn't look or act like the other wives on the block. For one thing, she almost never changed out of her nightgown, and sometimes wore it all day. And she rarely did any housework, and even though she spent the majority of her time in the kitchen, she absolutely never cooked, NEVER!

Eileen Smith never did one iota of anything in that house, nada. The only thing that woman ever did in that house was sit at the kitchen table eating bennies and valium's, drinking tea that was mostly sugar and cream, and reading stories about triumph's and hero's in monthly's like Ellery Queen and Readers Digest.

Some philosophers believe that there is a thin line that divides a hero from a zero.

For Eileen Smith, that thin line is more like a brick wall that she is on the wrong side of.

In Charles Smith's mind, heroism is limitless. A perfect example of that hero mentality, is how one Saturday morning, Charles and William were at the local farmers market getting some groceries. The area where the cash register was situated at, was just an enclosure that was open on both ends. They were next in line to pay for their groceries, when a large Doberman Pincher with a spiked collar wandered into the enclosure. William was just inches behind his father as the customer in front of them was leaving the counter. The dog approached William, and with a barely audible growl, it reared up on its hind legs, like it was going to attack him. In a flash, with his right hand clenched into a fist and turned inwards, Charles took half a step backwards and grabbed that dog by the neck and slung it so hard between him and the counter, that the animal itself, didn't make a sound as it landed with a "flop" in the corner. Snapped its neck instantly.

After paying for his groceries, Charles put a 50 dollar bill on the counter and mumbled "for the mutt".

And that was that, not one person said anything to Charles, one way or the other. even the dogs owner had nothing to say. Probably had enough sense to realize that it was his own damn fault that his beloved pet was gone.

That Saturday morning left a huge impression on William, his dad was larger than life, most definitely, the most important person in Williams world. To this day, William Smith loves his father UNCONDITIONALY.

If anyone reading this true story, thinks its almost over, forget it, not even close. As a matter of fact, Eileen Smith is just getting started. And anyone hoping for a happy ending for the Smith family, might as well put this book down right now, 'cause the ending is not a happy one.

For the souls that are willing tough it out till the end, now might be a good time to buckle your safety belt.

CHAPTER TWENTYFIVE

Around the time William turned 10, he noticed that his mothers demeanor changed drastically. She was more subdued, concentrating on something, like she had a big test to take the next day.

January 2, 1981 was a Tuesday. It was also the first day back to school for the Smith children. The day started just like hundreds of mornings did before this one came along. Charles would be first to rise out of bed, and leave for work almost an hour before anyone else had to get out of bed and start their day.

But that's where the similarity's end. The rest of this morning would be much, much different. As soon as Charles pulled out of the driveway, Eileen sprang out of bed, and in a mad rush, started to wake up all the children. Leslie went to the room that William and Brian shared and was helping little Brian get ready. Eileen ordered the others to gather up their Christmas stuff and all their clothes and get in the van that was parked out front.

"What's going on, where are we going?" William asked.

Leslie said, " wouldn't you rather go on a trip, than go to school today?"

William didn't know what to think. Eileen Jr came into his room and snapped, "just do what your mother tells you, you stupid fucker"

So William Relunctily gathered up all his things and got into the passenger van that was out front.

He assumed that maybe they were going upstate to visit his grandma Mae. But he didn't recall anyone talk about a trip anywhere and became very concerned about what was going on. The van made its way through Queens, then across the bridge to Manhattan and headed towards Grand Central.

And when the van turned into the same bus station parking lot that started the trip to California, years ago, a wave of fear came over William like he never felt before. He was very confused and didn't have his first clear thought until he was already in his seat, on the bus. And William thought to himself, " does dad know about this?"

For William, this bus trip across the United States, with his wanna-be brother and sisters, was almost exactly like the first one, except with 3 major differences, in order of importance, least to most.

First up, is the whirlwind, trailer park romance that unfolded during the middle part of the trip. Somewhere near Little Rock, Arkansas, The man wearing the cowboy hat, got on the bus, and sat in the same row of seats, across the aisle from William. His hat was an off white color, with a deep tan leather hat band. He was wearing some skin tight Wranglers, and an off white, long sleeve, button down, shirt, with dark tan pinstripes, to match the hat. The shirt collar was tied with a beautiful gold and black opal bola tie. His boots were of the finest craft, white washed, with shiny brass tips, and heel protectors. But it was his belt buckle that really stood out. The thing was HUGE, about the size of a salad plate. It was solid silver and had a 24kt gold rope border, with 2 big polished brass block letters,

B and H, a person could rightly assume the letters stood for BIG HOSS.

Mrs. Lot lizard got on the bus just a couple of stops after the man wearing the cowboy hat. She wasn't wearing much, just a white mini, mini skirt, with a white, "wife beater", tank top. No bra, so the outline of her light pink nipples were easy for anyone to see.

William always preferred the window seat, which left the seat next to him empty. And that's exactly where Mrs. Lot lizard sat. She immediately starts flirting with the man wearing the cowboy hat. He had a witty and charming character, and easily matched her dialog

Most likely, this man was just being polite, there was no way he would ever choose this woman for a mate. Mrs. Lot lizard, on the other hand, thought that she had just found her next victim. She was already plotting how to get this man to give her all his money.

Somewhere in Texas, the bus driver informed the passengers that there would be at least a 45 minute layover at the next stop, so people could stretch out their legs and whatnot.

When the bus pulled into the station, William saw the man wearing the cowboy hat hand Mrs. Lot lizard a C-note($100) and told her "go down the street to White Castle, and get us a couple of those burgers, ok."

"ok, sugar." And off she went.

About an hour later, Mrs. Lot lizard makes a appearance across the street, at a gas station. She is on the back of some guys motorcycle, hanging all over this guy, kissing on his neck and stuff.

William was already in his seat when the man wearing the cowboy hat sat in his. William wondered if he had seen Mrs. Lizard yet, and said to the man, "hey mister, isn't that the lady over there that was supposed to get you something to eat?" William was pointing across the street.

The man stood up out of his seat, looked over at what William was pointing at and said, "why, I think your right, young man." And then sat right back down.

William was confused, a $100 was a lot of money, so he said to the man, "well, aren't you going to ask her about your money?"

With that, the man wearing the cowboy hat burst out laughing, laughing uncontrollably, to the point he had to hold his gut.

As the bus pulled out of the station, and the man was still laughing, William noticed that Mrs. Lizard was now arguing with the man on the motorcycle. As the bus got further from the station, Mrs. Lizard started chasing the bus hooting and hollering, waving her arms.

The man wearing the cowboy hat shouted at the driver, "hey bud, there's a $100 in it for you, if you just ignore that woman, and keep driving, what do you say?" and the bus picked up speed.

The man wearing the cowboy hat let out a sigh of relief, and said, "boy, that was a close one."

Still confused William said, "but what about your $100 bucks?"

The man wearing the cowboy hat looked William right in the eye, and with a more serious tone in his voice said, "you see young man, I don't think you really understand, but I got exactly what I paid for, as a matter of fact, a hundred dollars is a mighty fair price to pay, to get rid of a varmint like that!"

The man pulled out another hundred dollar bill and a ten, and handed them both to William and said " now you go give that C-note to the driver and you can have the 10 bucks, ok?"

"OK"

The next big difference between the two trips, was that even though he never bothered to read his ticket, William knew in his heart that this trip was one way, and that he wouldn't see his father or New York City, for a long, long time.

But the biggest, and likely most important difference between these two trips is the fanfare they are met with upon arriving in the same farming community as back in '77.

There were 2 network affiliated news crews already at the bus station, waiting to do this story about this poor abused housewife, and her 5 abused and neglected children, and how she escaped the clutches of this monster of a husband and made the harrowing cross country journey to safety.

100%, undeniable, complete, and total BULLSHIT!!!

By far the biggest lie that ABC, and CBS HAVE EVER AIRED!!!

If the real truth had been aired that January night so long ago, it would have been a story about a woman from New York that just kidnapped 5 people from a safe and loving home, followed by a picture and a F.B.I. BOLO (be on look out) for Eileen Smith, not considered to be armed, but most definitely dangerous.

The evening of January 2nd 1981 was Charles very own personal Pearl Harbor, a deliberate sneak attack.

As soon as he turned onto the block, he knew something wasn't right, the house was completely dark. When he pulled into the driveway, he began to worry. No TV blaring from the living room. None of his kids running around doing whatever it is that they do.

Nothing, when he went inside, there was not a soul in sight.

Charles Smith came home to an empty house that day, no warning, no note, not even a phone call after the fact. Wife and 5 kids, gone, just like that, poof!, disappeared like a fart in the wind. And for many years, had no idea were they went. One can only imagine the pain and anguish that Charles suffered when his family left, and NEVER came back.

A person of ANY stature, would be hard pressed, to be able to, find ANYONE, in this whole world, that could say, Charles Smith, deserved to have that done to him. No William, your dad didn't know.

A MEANS TO AN END

CHAPTER TWENTYSIX

New York City and central California's San Joaquin Valley are as opposite as opposite can get, with one of these locations surrounded by mountains, and the other surrounded by water. Just about everything was opposite, even to the point that when someone said "Bad", it meant good.

Relocating to California from New York City at 10 years old, was one of the hardest things William has ever had to do. It was a lot like he was from the moon, then moved to the sun, crashing and burning upon arrival.

It would be Williams NY accent that would cause him the most grief. His accent was strong, with a "wuah" type of sound to certain words like qwuahter(quarter),or wuahter(water). The teasing was relentless, kids can be really cruel to each other.

Not long after arriving in California, Leslie, Eileen Jr, and Ted, one by one, go out on their own. Leslie was first, just days after getting off the bus. Eileen Jr left just weeks later, Ted hung in there almost 6 months. Eileen Sr just let them go, left them to their own devices, left to run amuck on the streets of this farming community, this hick town, in central California. The leaders and elected officials of this hick town like to think of their town as a big city. Not even close, this farming community is just that, a farming community, nothing more. Just another hick town in the heartland of America.

Its worth noting that this hick town, has another, smaller, hick town, literally attached to it.

A well respected, worldwide, news organization recently did a short non-feature article about this "smaller hick town", claiming it to be, by far, hands down, the best place on the planet, to raise a family.

The victimization at the "hands" of Chad, happened right there in that "smaller hick town". And, in the very near future, William will be victimized two more times, in that same "smaller hick town"

Rock solid proof, that no community is immune to society's woe's, no matter what a magazine might claim.

With the 3 older Smith children out of the house already, Eileen didn't need too big of a dwelling, to accommodate her two youngest and herself. She ended up renting a run down 2 bedroom apartment, in a low overhead, high crime neighborhood.

She barely provided the basics, clothing was second hand or donated. Eileen didn't care how her kids looked or if they fit in with the other kids, some of the things she provided them to wear to school were hideous, nobody in their right mind would send their kids out dressed like Eileen sent her two boys out.

Eileen continued to ignore William, never teaching him anything, purposely leaving him without the necessary information needed to succeed in society, and stay safe. Basic knowledge every parent share's with their kids, so those kids don't end up being victimized, in what has always been, a very dangerous world.

By purposely not educating her son, has given him a naïve, very meek character, easy to fool and manipulate. So its no surprise, that the many predators that walk among us in society, found William an easy target.

In contrast, Eileen's next potential victim, was made aware of, by this mans youngest son.

Actually, its quite admirable, the way she meets the next man in her life.

It was a hot summer afternoon, and Eileen was walking with William and his brother Brian, along the downtown mall. She was there for an appointment with social service's, trying to procure benefits of some kind, when all of the sudden, a Mexican boy the same age as William, ran past the trio a few feet, then turned around with his hand up, like a traffic cop, and said, "excuse me lady, but my dad really wants to meet you, and he has really bad knee's, so he sent me to ask you if you'll wait for him to catch up."

"Oh really, your not kidding me, are you?" Eileen was intrigued to say the least.

"naw', lady, he walks with a cane. Will you wait for him?" he asked.

"Ok, I'll wait under the shade of that tree right over there, ok?" she answered.

Maybe 15 or 20 seconds had passed, when the Mexican boy said, "here he comes now!"

Gilbert Fernando, and his youngest son, Andy. Andy has 2 older brothers, 1 older sister. Gilbert Jr is next oldest, sister Aurora, and oldest son, Dezi.

They were instantly smitten with each other, and Gil, as he is liked to be called, asked her out to dinner. Eileen accepted, and he decided to take her to very popular Basque restaurant. A kid friendly environment, so having her boys with her wasn't a problem. Gil allowed Andy to head home by himself, Andy not wanting to be a part of this "date".

As her boys sat at a different table, each with a glass of water in front of them, Eileen acted out her broken housewife role to perfection. And how she moved here from New York to get away from his imaginary abuse. This gave them a lot in common, Gil being divorced himself, a single parent raising a handful of kids. It was most likely the pinnacle of his interest in her. He viewed her to be much like himself, a single parent, struggling to make ends meet, with no outside help.

That first date went really well for both of these Adults, and the relationship got serious almost instantly. Eileen would leave her boys at home alone once a week or so to go visit Gil at his home on the west side of this farming community, a notoriously dangerous neighborhood.

One Saturday afternoon, William was at the local 7-eleven, by himself, purchasing a snack of some kind, pretzels most likely.

As William exited the store, an older gentleman was sitting in his car, as though he was waiting for someone. William glanced up as he walked passed this mans car. The man said to William, "hey there young man, would like to go to (fast food restaurant) and get something to eat?"

Enter into Williams life, one Carlos J Pedophile. This guy has to be the iconic image of what child predators look like. He's driving a '69 Chevrolet station wagon, faded yellow with these half rusted moon hubcaps on the wheels. He's wearing grey slacks with blue and grey New Balance tennis shoes with bright fluorescent green accents. A short sleeve button down shirt with some stripe pattern. Almost completely bald, topped off with some wire rim eyeglasses, complete with some "to cool for school" flip-down shades.

"Ok, sure", the simple fact that nobody ever warned William about the many dangers in the world, and add in that William hadn't had a decent meal since leaving New York, made this predators tactics, sure fire.

And when this hook of a meal, baited with a chocolate milkshake was over, Mr. Pedophile insisted on giving William a ride home, actually he was adamant about it. He told William that he wanted to meet Williams parents, so that, as he put it, "we can do this again".

That's when William told Carlos that his father didn't live with them. And how they just moved here from New York, but their father stayed behind.

"Ok, I guess, lets go" William said as he got back into the wagon.

Upon arriving at the apartments where William lived with his mother, William jumped out of the wagon first and jogged to the door and left that door open for his new friend.

As soon as Eileen heard her son enter the apartment, she started interrogating her son, "where have you been? You haven't been talking to your father, have you?" she was always worried about William having contact with his father, something she forbid William from doing.

"No mom, this nice man took me to (fast food restaurant) for dinner." William said while jerking his thumb over his shoulder, like Carlos was standing behind him.

"What man, are you lying to me?" she said

"He must have waited at the door" William guessed correctly. Carlos was waiting at the door, waiting to be invited in, just like a vampire that must be invited, before he's allowed to enter his next victims dwelling.

Carlos is met with a lackluster, "oh, hello, come on in, and thank you so much for taking that kid out to eat."

"It was my pleasure, my name is Carlos, and…………"

Carlos goes on to tell Eileen how an old war wound has prevented him from having kids of his own, bla, bla, bla. And how he just wants to make under-privileged kids happy, bla, bla, bla. And then Carlos asked Eileen, "are there any other children in the home that I can help out?"

To which Eileen answered, "well, there's little Brian."

Carlos added, "oh, really, and how old is Brian?"

Eileen answered, "8"

And the very next thing that came out of this creeps mouth was, "AWESOME"

Then, as if on cue, Carlos followed Eileen to the kitchen and sat opposite from her at the kitchen table. William was then told to go outside and play.

Eileen does the unthinkable, "why yes, you can take the boys out to eat anytime you like." The woman, knowingly or un-knowingly, just handed her two youngest sons, over to a pedophile.

It started out with weekly trips to fast food restaurants, and ice cream parlors. It soon moved up to these once a month shopping spree's, affording William and his brother things they wouldn't have had other wise. Things like expensive shoes and clothes. Skateboards, video games, bicycles.

And don't think that Eileen was just going to let this "nice man" spend hundreds of dollars a month on her kids, and not get her cut. You could be as sure that the sun was going to rise everyday, that Eileen was compensated as well.

So a person might ask the question, "so where does this guy get all this money, to throw around like it grew on trees?"

Well, as it turns out, Carlos J Pedophile is REALLY good at making wine, so good at it, he gets paid very, very well to teach other people how to make it.

Guess his money grows on VINES !!!

CHAPTER TWENTYSEVEN

William and his brother Brian would soon be spending every weekend at Carlos J Pedophile's apartment in that "even smaller hick town" mentioned before.

Late One Saturday night, while Carlos was working on his computer that was in his bedroom, William had fallen asleep in the recliner, in the living room while he was watching TV. Little Brian stayed home for some reason.

William was alone.

About 1 am, Carlos came to the living room and woke William up, saying, "you would probably be more comfortable on the floor, so you can stretch out"

William thought maybe Carlos wanted to sit in his recliner and watch TV. So William made a little mat on the floor and laid down to go back to sleep. Carlos, instead of sitting in the recliner or going back to his room, laid down on the floor, almost ln top of him. Carlos then begins humping Williams leg and groping his buttocks.

This came so far out of left field, its no wonder William froze with fear, and that's not the reaction Carlos wanted. Carlos is getting frustrated and growled," I give you fuckers a lot of love, how come I cant get some loving from you little shitheads!" The leg humping became desperate and Carlos finally rolled off William and yelled, "its not fair" before he slammed his bedroom door.

William got very lucky that night, lucky that Carlos was unable to attain an erection. Maybe he was getting to old, or maybe it was that William was older than he liked them. Whatever the case, if Carlos had been able to get it up that night, William would have surely been raped.

The relationship between Gil and Eileen was becoming stagnant, loosing its honeymoon type of appeal.

Eileen was spending almost all of her time at Gil's and he already knew the 3 older kids were out on their own for awhile now, but he wondered about the two younger smith boys and why they were never with her.

"Where are your boys? Who's watching them?" he asked.

"Oh, their fine, an old family friend is watching them, their just fine" Eileen stated.

JUST FINE?

A predator that lives right across the street from Carlos just started a conversation with William about bicycles, then waterbed creep invites William into his apartment for something cold to drink. Once inside, waterbed creep hands William a Zima of all things. The next thing waterbed creep did was put some educational programing (pornography) on the TV. And if all that wasn't bad enough, creep gave William some COCAINE!!!

So here's 10 year old William Smith, slightly drunk, high as a kite, and has been watching people cum all over the place for the past 20 minutes. In a low voice, waterbed creep said to William, "hey, you want to cum like the people in the movie?"

William remembered Chad using that word years ago and when creep said it, Williams already erect penis started throbbing and he answered, "hell yes!"

With that, creep pointed towards his bedroom. William actually and instantly had a mental picture of at least one naked woman waiting for them in his room. So William followed waterbed creep down a short hallway to his bedroom to find that, nope, no naked lady, just an empty WATERBED. William was a little disappointed. Creep then begged William to let him give William a blow job. William was kind of apprehensive, but creep pleaded with and convinced William to let him suck his dick. Trust and believe that this orgasm felt a hundred times better than the time Chad did it to him.

Then creep asked William if he could fuck him in the ass, to which William replied, "HELL NO!" Creep then climbed on top of William, humped on his stomach a few times and blew his wad all over Williams chest.

No woman, their not "just fine", one of your sons was "just molested"

And lets not forget Williams parting gift from waterbed creep, why it's a shiny, brand spanking new drug habit. A big thank you to everybody that made this tragedy possible. Couldn't have happened without their help. So thanks again,.........FOR NOTHING

There's a good reason that thousands of victims just like William, NEVER told anyone what these men were doing to them, if it was you, yes you reading this story, would you want to tell anyone about some fucked up weirdo shit that was done to you??? No you wouldn't.

If a study was done, and a hundred men and women were asked if they remembered their first orgasm, 97 of them would have to admit that, yes they do remember their first orgasm. And 94 of those people based their whole entire sexuality, on that first orgasm. Unfortunately for some of us, that first orgasm was the result of a selfish, uncaring adult, TRESSPASSING on our sexuality. Sad but true.

CHAPTER TWENTYEIGHT

The relationship between Eileen and Gil started showing cracks in its foundation, the single parent allure.

Gil was starting to realize that Eileen was not really a caring, loving parent. As far as he could tell, she wasn't actually raising her boys at all, someone else was doing it. And she didn't interact very well with his two sons either. It almost seemed like she had never even been a parent. She didn't clean or cook, and that was one of his biggest issues with this woman, cooking. As with any food preference, from the many different cultures around the world, it is especially important in Latino culture, that the person doing the cooking not only knows what their doing, but does it with the right pizzas', the right oomph'.

Gil desperately tried to show her how to cook, to no avail. She had absolutely no desire to do very much of anything, for anyone! Let alone, cook for a bunch of people on a regular basis.

There are Women in this world that dedicate every waking moment of their precious lives, to making sure that their family has something nutritious, and delicious, to eat, everyday. God bless these Women.

Gil was also put off by her extreme gambling habit, even though he liked to gamble a little himself, betting on horse's and sports, Eileen took it to the extreme, sometimes making twice a week trips to the nearest Indian casino.

But by far, the biggest issue was marriage. Gil was raised in a very traditional setting, marriage being a big part of life in Latino culture. Gil wanted to put a ring on this woman's finger and make her his wife when the relationship first started.

Eileen was still married to Charles, and absolutely refused to grant him a divorce.

"You say he's this big, giant piece of shit, right, well, if he is such a dirt bag, why then you wont divorce him?" he asked her.

"Never you mind, its none of your business!" she told him. She had a specific reason for never granting Charles a divorce, it was a major part of her plan.

Williams new cocaine habit, on top of a marijuana habit would cause a myriad of problems for him, starting with Carlos. As soon as William started doing drugs, Carlos was aware of it. One of his earlier victims started doing drugs also, so he knew all the signs that made it apparent William was using.

And Mr. Pedophile was very anti-drug, they interfered with his agenda concerning young boys. To Carlos, smoking a little reefer, and snorting a few (hundred thousand) lines makes a person the biggest piece of poop in the world. But sodomizing little boys??? THAT'S A-OK !!!

So William started spending less and less time at Carlos's apartment, until pretty soon, William stopped visiting Carlos altogether.

As his drug use increased, so did the amount of time he spent away from home, running around with all kinds of different kids from the neighborhood. William had lots of girl friends, he was handsome and tall for his age.

It would be very easy to assume that William was overcompensating his heterosexuality due to the abuse he was exposed to, before and during puberty.

Even though William never had enough self esteem to know this about himself, but many girls, and even women, found him to be very handsome. This made it very easy for William to lose his virginity, and relatively young, losing it right before he turned 14. As a matter of fact, the girl he lost his virginity to, happened to be of African descent. She was a year older than William and she is the one who pursued William, relentlessly. Apprehensive in the beginning because of the difference in respective culture's, he declined her first two offers, but the third time this girl literally threw herself at him, William's carnal desires got the best of him and has sex with her one afternoon, after school. Leaving out the specific details, he enjoyed it way more than her.

And that really didn't bother this girl in the least, her intention's were not motivated by passion. Her reasons were deception. A couple of weeks after this encounter, this girl came to William and told him that she was pregnant, and that he was the father, but not to worry, she would be having an abortion.

#1 she really was pregnant, but she already knew William wasn't the father.

#2 she never planned on getting an abortion

Her goal was to protect the real fathers identity, mostly so he wouldn't have to pay child support. She told everyone William was the father.

She started receiving financial assistance even before the baby was born, which caused Eileen to receive a notice that her son owes child support, and that she would be responsible for the payments until William turned 18.

Eileen was besides herself, she wasn't even aware that William was sexually active, something that was a major concern to her evil plot. Eileen insisted on a paternity test, on a hunch. And her instincts were right, William was not the father, and they were off the hook for the support.

Eileen was still very concerned about William having sex with girls, and she actually forbid him from doing so, stating that he was too young. She even went as far as to threaten William with violence, and even sent Eileen Jr's husband, William's brother-in-law Jerry and his brother Ted out to rough William up in an effort to scare William away from girls.

Didn't work, only made William try to have sex with as many girls as possible. If William ended up having a son, it would destroy the ground work Eileen has spent the past 20 years implementing.

Eileen succeeded in making sure she abused Theodore enough in the womb to make him sterile, Ted had been married for several years and no children. Ultimately, Ted was never able to father any children. But Eileen was not as sure with William. Charles did well to keep her drinking to a minimum during Williams time in the womb.

To Eileen's disappointment, William did get one of these girls pregnant, and the girl chose to have the baby. William would leave home, drop out of high school, and go to work full time. He became a teenage parent and did his best to be a husband and father to this girl and their new baby.

And wouldn't you know it, William had a son. Eileen was extremely upset at this development, and would have to scrap her original plan, and somehow come up with a plan B.

CHAPTER TWENTYNINE

William did his best to do right by his girlfriend and their son, but this toxic relationship would only last 6 months before they went their separate ways, the girl friend retaining custody of the child.

Mean while, Leslie Smith, after separating from her husband, and the father of her two sons, James and Jack, enters into a whirlwind relationship with a young German immigrant, and quickly gives birth to a baby girl. And even though at the time this child was born, Leslie's legal last name was Danberry, and the German father's last name was Goff, Leslie named her daughter Helen Eileen Smith, that's right, another Eileen Smith. It was something Eileen Sr ordered Leslie to do, which now made Leslie a wiling participant in her mothers wicked scheme.,

When William broke ties with his sons mother, he ended up spending most of his time at Leslie's, he was like a live in babysitter. He had a front row seat to this spontaneous relationship with this young German man, saw first hand how this man was a doting father, changing diapers, doing his part. William never understood why all of the sudden this doting father, 5 months after Helen Eileen Smith was born, this man just up and disappears, leaving his daughter, never to return. It wasn't until many years later that William would learn of this German mans fate.

This now made William very useful around Leslie's home, becoming a paid caretaker of Leslie's kids while she attended a local community collage. She knew good and well her kids were safe in his care.

Although, there was one very close call. Per the normal routine, after Leslie left for school, the kids would be fed, and then William would let the three of them, 6 year old James, 4 year old Jack, and of course, Helen, who was a toddler still in diapers, outside to play in the courtyard that was surrounded by the apartment buildings. William would usually sit in a chair in the courtyard to keep a close eye on them. As they played in the courtyard, for whatever reason, William went into the apartment, he was inside for less than 90 seconds, and when he returned, the 3 children were gone! In a panic William ran to the front of the complex, to the street and searched in vain, after checking both side streets, he went back to the courtyard and began knocking on doors, asking if anyone had seen the children.

By now it had been over 30 minutes since William had eyes on his niece and nephews. Behind the apartments were a set of very busy rail road tracks, and on the other side of the tracks was a large sports complex that had an Olympic sized diving pool.

The neighbor that answered the last door William knocked on, suggested that he look behind the apartments. During his search of the alley, he noticed a spilled can of white paint. When he reached the train tracks, he finally spotted the trio. To Williams horror, the three were inside the fenced in diving pool, James held one of his little sisters arms, and Jack held the other, and they were dunking her in and out of the deep end of the pool. It looked as if they were trying to drown her.

William thought "oh no, they killed their little sister" as he jumped the fence, grabbed Helen away from her brother and made sure she was still alive. Then with the baby in one arm, literally spanked the oldest all the way back to the apartment with the other.

After his arm tired out from spanking the crap out of this kid, William screamed, "what the fuck were you jackasses doing to your sister?"

They told their uncle that they were playing in the alley and spilled paint on their sister and were trying to remove the paint by using the pool like a gigantic tub. The outcome could have been much worse. KIDS.

During this same time period, Eileen realized that there was no big payday on the horizon in this relationship with Gil. Just like someone addicted to heroin, a gambling junkies craving for money to gamble with is just as intense.

The lengths people will go through to get their "fix", are incredible to say the least, and sometimes very violent. This is when Eileen decides to victimize a local grocery store. With her youngest, Brian in tow, she entered the store and went straight to the produce aisle and pretends to be shopping until she is the only customer in the aisle. Eileen then takes a tomato and smashes it ln the floor. She then gently laid on top of it and called out for help, faking a hip injury.

She would later claim in court that the store was responsible for her injury's, because they neglected to clean the aisle.

And a civil judge agreed, to the tune of tens of thousands of dollars. To this day, that woman hasn't so much as broken a fingernail.

Eileen would then burn through that money, like a late summer grass fire.

Less than a year and a half later, Eileen attempted to do the same thing to another grocery store, but for some reason was unsuccessful this time. She was subsequently denied disability assistance. Eileen Smith is solely responsible for the difficulty's people face when they get hurt for real, and try to collect rightfully earned disability.

But fear not devil worshipers and hate mongers, the next felony Eileen commits and gets away with is just around the corner, not far over the next horizon.

CHAPTER THIRTY

I t wasn't always smooth sailing In the boat that was the living arrangement between William and Leslie. Sometimes their were disagreements that became heated arguments. Leslie would occasionally kick William out, leaving William with little choice of places to shelter. His mothers place was out of the question, after he had his son, Eileen now detested her already hated son, William.

William did have one other option, Eileen Jr and his brother in law, Jerry. The second time William had a falling out with Leslie, he went to make his usual plea to Eileen Jr. But when he got there, Jerry informed William that Eileen Jr had travelled to New York.

"she went to visit dad?" William asked.

Jerry said, "no, she went to Valley Stream to take care of something for your mom."

"What?"

Jerry replied, " something about your moms foster parents, I think they died, and your sister is taking care of their estate"

William was too naïve to realize that what his brother in law just told him, makes not one bit of sense. Never would the granddaughter be appointed to be executor of an estate inherited by the daughter.

"She will be back in a couple of days, you can stay if you need to" Jerry said. The man is a righteous soul, and took a liking to William. Even took William under his wing for a brief period.

When Eileen Jr finally returned from New York, she was very excited about what she had just done. When William asked her what was so great about it, Eileen Jr stated, "oh, I had to wait a couple of days before Mrs. Uncino passed, then mom told me to sell all their stuff and bring her the money, they had a lot of jewelry, and antiques, I had a blast."

The truth as to why Eileen Jr went to New York was because Mr. Uncino had died, but Mrs. Uncino was in excellent shape and most likely would live for a number of years. Eileen Sr wasn't going to wait any longer than she could stand on one leg to get her hands on the Uncino fortune. And this is part of the reason why Eileen Jr is named as such, so she could present herself as Eileen Sr and do things for her mother, like murder Mrs. Uncino, then pretend to be the grieving daughter and make sure Mrs. Uncino is cremated as soon as possible. AND, this was just a dress rehearsal for Eileen Jr, the real act is yet to come.

Eileen Sr would then sell the Uncino's $800,000 property, for less than $329,000, taking a half a MILLION dollar loss. She thinks she's smart, but in reality, she just might have the I.Q. of a rat.

It was during this time that William, oblivious to what his sisters where getting involved in, began to gain an enormous amount of respect for both of his sisters. Mostly, William could see that they always put their children first. On top of that, if a husband or boyfriend was abusive, or lazy, or not up to par in any way, down the road they went. Neither of these women put up with very much bullshit from the men in their lives'.

The bouncing back and forth between his two sisters would not last forever, and he was also bouncing around between a few different fast food jobs, jobs that don't really have much of a future.

William also had a strong desire to visit his dad in New York, and when he turned 18, quit his job at some burger joint, told both of his sisters, who were dependent on William as a babysitter, thanks for everything. He then boarded a bus heading east, he was finally going home, going home to tell his dad that he loves him and he's sorry over what Eileen did to him.

Charles was very happy his favorite kid took it upon himself to be the first one to return to New York. The seven year mystery was finally solved. Charles finally learned the truth about what happened that day, back in '81.

And Charles picked up right were he left off, trying to mold his second oldest son into a man, but was already robbed of that opportunity. The intentional neglect and downright abuse, William suffered at the hands of his own mother, had solidified, William's already meek and naïve character.

Father and son made the best of their situation and got along very well for the 2 years William resided in New York. And Charles was pleased when William, within 2 weeks, found a good job as a machine operator in a factory that manufactured wall paper. William held on to that job for the whole time he stayed in New York, but due to circumstances beyond his control, would lose that job just 2 months shy of 2 years.

Actually, it was a very surreal experience, almost horrifying. There were 120 other employees on Williams shift. It happened to be payday when right before lunch, all 120 workers were called into the break room for an emergency meeting, then all 120 workers were handed pink slips, told that they didn't have jobs anymore. No warning, no two week severance pay, NOTHING! Some of these people had been working at this factory since it opened 30+ years ago. Depended on this job to make their mortgage payment and put food on the table.

People were in shock, carrying on and crying and shouting, and it turned into pandemonium, almost a riot.

A recently hired employee that owned his own business, a growing security company, hired 40 people on the spot. This company would go on to become one of the biggest private security firms in New York, ultimately hiring over 100 of the people that lost their jobs that day. God bless that man for turning a tragedy, into a triumph.

William decided it would be easier to find work out in California, where at the time, the new housing industry was booming, with no end in sight. Add in the fact that he knew he could always get help from Leslie, made the decision even easier.

Parting on good terms with his father, William headed back to California to find work in the construction industry.

When William arrived in California, both of his sisters were at the bus station, waiting for him, competing with each other to see who would be having their favorite babysitter's services. There was another reason that his sisters were waiting for him, they were ordered by Eileen Sr to welcome William back, and find out if William had obtained any information she didn't want him to have. He didn't, William was completely oblivious to the evil plot, that now put the target on his back. This would be the beginning of one of the biggest betrayal's, that almost anyone in HISTORY, has ever faced.

Even from childhood, William never really got along well with Eileen Jr, and would prefer to lodge with his sister, Leslie. In William's mind, and for that matter, the appearance to outsiders, is that a bond was forming between these two particular siblings.

Even though both of his sisters offered shelter, William chose Leslie, and temporarily resumed babysitting for her. He was upfront with her about his desire to get into construction, a real mans job, building stuff, just like his father. She actually scoffed at the notion, probably not wanting to loose his services.

CHAPTER THIRTYONE

In a few months, William would accept an offer from his best friend from high school, for work in residential construction. Leslie was not happy about this development and his new career caused problems between them. Eventually, William struck out on his own, starting a career in construction, that lasted 26 years.

Over the years, William would see less and less of his siblings, get together's, and visits would eventually stop altogether. Except with Leslie, William always kept in contact with her throughout the years. And he most definitely called his father way more than he called Eileen, even though she lives in the same town.

William rose through the ranks in the construction world rather quickly, and did well for himself. He wasn't rich, but wasn't poor either.

William spent most of his spare time with the high school friend that gave him his first job, even though William no longer worked for him. They went fishing, and hunting, always drunk and stoned, it's a miracle they never hurt anybody or themselves.

And just like most things in life, all good things in life, eventually come to an end. William and his high school friend would have a falling out over a relationship William had started with his future wife, Stephanie. As the relationship with Stephanie got serious, William spent almost all of his spare time with her, never making time for his old friend.

Its crazy, some of the things that adolescents and young adults do, trouble we get into in the prime of our lives. After staying up all night drinking and doing drugs, Stephanie made a kind of agreement with William, she told William that if him and a friend of his could lift 2 cases of beer from a gas station, she would be willing to go to a grocery store and steal a large bottle of whisky. William and his friend agreed, and they chose a gas station that was unique when it came to how and where the register and cashier were located. They were behind bullet proof glass, in an enclosure, which made it very easy for someone to just walk out with pretty much whatever they like.

With the beer run out of the way, it was Stephanie's turn, which took place at a nearby grocery store. Once she had obtained the whisky, William followed Stephanie to the check out line with a deck of cards and a lemon. When William tried to pay for the items, the store manager approached them and reached out, in attempt to restrain Stephanie, saying, "I want the bottle of booze in your purse!"

William reached around Stephanie and slapped the managers arm out of the way. Stephanie then ducked under the managers other arm, and ran to the exit.

William tried to push past the store manager, at which point he punched William in the eye, William responded with a upward elbow to the side of the managers head and tried to make it to the exit. Several other employees would come to their bosses aid, and tackle William before he made it to the exit. Once they had him on the ground, they kicked him a couple of times, making sure that they were able to hold him until the police arrived. Stephanie was long gone, escaped, scott free with the loot from the mornings activity's.

William was charged with assault, and robbery two. Unable to afford a lawyer, William pleaded to the charges and was sentenced to 1 year in county jail, leniency given because it was his first offense.

William served 9 and half months of the twelve, and to his surprise, when he was released, Stephanie was waiting for him with the bottle of booze and two cases of beer, the very same ones from 9 months ago

William was very impressed, and would eventually marry this woman. William also fathered a daughter while he was married to Stephanie. Just like before, with his first child, William did his best to do right by his wife and daughter. At first things seemed to be going well for this new family, but some problems started to become apparent. It started with Stephanie, she was self conscious about the way she looked. On top of being tall, she was a little overweight, and this caused her to be kind of frigid in the bedroom.

It was also during this time that William would have some doubts about his sexuality, experimenting with an alternative lifestyle.

All of these things, plus some financial shortcomings would doom this marriage, ultimately ending in divorce. And just like before, Stephanie would retain custody of the child.

The financial shortcomings just mentioned would have a big impact on William's life and career. For the first 19 years of his 26 years in the construction industry, William was on the contractor side of the fence, doing piece work and being his own boss.

The freedoms of the jobsite are unmatched, out of any other genre in the working world. Piece work was a pretty good deal also. It's when a worker assumes the role of a sub-contractor, doing a certain "piece" of the work. Let's say a painter gets paid $2800 to paint an entire house, whether it takes 2 days, or 10. Now, how many houses do you want to paint a week, just 1?, or 3? A person can make an enormous amount of money, in a short amount of time.

And that's how things went for William, for almost two decades, his best year contracting, he made close to 40,000 dollars, but just two years later, the housing industry hit a slump so hard, that William only made 17,000. It was that kind of instability and pressure from the builder William contracted with the most, that would cause him to make the biggest mistake of his entire career. William would jump to the job site management side of the fence, becoming a minion for this builder, ruining his reputation as a contractor and burning bridges along the way.

There were a series of events that led to William eventually quitting this adventure that turned into a nightmare. Starting with Peoples Ditch. The project William managed was about an hours drive from where he lives, and he made the commute on a daily basis. This project was bordered on one side by an irrigation canal called Peoples Ditch. The main road into this brand new neighborhood, dead ended with a barricade, as though sometime in the future, the road would continue on over and past the canal. People's Ditch is called that for a reason. It's not just one farmer that owns water rights to this canal, its several, like 5 or 6 different farmers depend on this waterway for their livelihood.

It was a Thursday morning, and William was driving down the highway, on his way to work. Just before he reached the job site, he got a call from his boss, Jim.

"hello"

There were never any pleasantry's with phone calls like this.

" hey William, you still in bed or what?" Jim asked

William said, "just turned into the neighborhood, what's up?"

Jim told William, "good, good, do me a favor and drive to the barricade"

Silence for the 15 or 20 seconds it took William to get to the barricade. He put his truck in park and said, "ok, now what?

Jim, "what do you see?"

William, "I see a barricade Jim"

"Are you still sitting in your truck?" Jim asked

" Yea, hold on" William said.

Jim didn't even give him enough time to walk over to the canal when he asked," what do you see?"

"I see a canal, Jim"

He told William, "what's in the canal?"

William responded, "nothing"

Jim said, "no water?"

"Not a drop" William said, and got a dial tone. It was simple mathematics for Jim, he could always depend on what William said to be truth.

William didn't give the call much thought, even though he was aware that his company had acquired the 110 acre corn field that was on the other side of the canal. As he went about his duties for the day, he didn't notice the semi that pulled into the neighborhood. It was towing a flat bed trailer with a excavator on it. The semi went straight to the barricade, unloaded the excavator, and knocked down the barricade. The excavator then proceeded to dig a 6 ft wide, 16 ft deep, 50 ft long TRENCH, right thru peoples ditch. WITHOUT PERMISION.

When the day was over, as William left his office, he was approached by a man who was obviously some kind of farmer. The man said, " are you the super for this tract?"

"Why yes sir I am." William answered.

Its hard to describe, but this mans face changed in an instant, the color of his face turned beet red, eyes went bloodshot, and several facial veins popped up, he then started screaming at William, "you sorry son of a bitch, just who do you think you are………." And how I was taking food out of his family's mouth and so on, and so on. The tirade lasted well over 3 minutes and only ended when this farmer threw his john deer ball cap at William, then charged at William with his fist clenched. William barely made it to his truck before this pissed off farmer could reach him and was trying to bust out William's window as he started his truck and sped off.

The EPA (environmental protection agency), the state police, and a couple of other agency's got involved in meting out punishment to Williams company, that included a $50,000 fine. But you know what got Jim back and hurt the company the most?

That pissed off farmer got his other farmer buddy to flood that cornfield for 6 weeks!!! Might as well have been 6 months.

Even monkey's know NOT to mess with farmers.

Next up, inspector bong hit Bill. One of the floorplans being built had a free standing fireplace in between the living room and the dining room. The flue went straight up through a vaulted ceiling. On the shear inspection, Bill didn't like the way the bracing was done for this chimney flue and wants it done differently.

William gets the ok to proceed, and Bill will check the repair that doesn't need to be done on the next inspection. This "repair" is done several more times, up until the drywall nailing inspection, where the repair was left exposed by leaving off that part of the sheetrock.

Bill took one look at this repair and mumbled "I still don't like that" and went to the garage and nailed a red "STOP WORK" notice to the wall and left.

William told the drywall guys, who were in the garage waiting for the inspection to pass, " TAPE IT, and hang that fucking piece of drywall above the fireplace!!!" and took that red card and defiantly tore it in half.

William felt that Bill was abusing his power, and being unreasonable. The most likely reason for Bill's actions, is that even though he knows his way around a job site, he might not fully understand blueprints, and was looking at something he had never seen before.

About an hour later, the inspector returned to the house in question with two police cruisers in tow. William ran from his office to this house, and when he walked into the garage the police were telling the drywall guys to vacate the house or go to jail. One of the two officers there said to Bill, "is this my suspect?"

Bill responded, "sure is"

The officer, " sir, turn around and put your hands behind your back, your under arrest, you have the right to……."

William was handcuffed, put in the back of one of the cruisers, and taken downtown. He was booked, put in a cell, and held for 5 hours. Then William was released, cited out of jail, with a "disobeying a civil order" charge. When he finally got to the job site where his truck was parked, it was past 9 pm.

William immediately called Jim, "already heard about it bud, can't talk about it right now, and you better be at the main office first thing in the morning!" the next thing William heard was dial tone.

William knew right then and there, he was going to get fired. When he got home that night, he just couldn't relax. Didn't get much sleep either, tossing and turning all night.

On his way to the office the next morning, he thought, " on my way to pick up my last check, shoot." But to Williams amazement, when he walked through the door, all the office workers started clapping, and cheering. Someone even whistled.

Jim was no where in sight, but the owner of this multi-billion dollar company comes out of his office, arms open wide, and told William, "hey William, come on over here, let me take you out to lunch!"

When William got to Steve's office, he said, "I'm not fired?"

Steve said, "FIRED?!, no, no, son your not fired, heck, I'm kind of impressed,…." Steve then put his arm around Williams shoulder and said, "I think you did a great job yesterday, that's how you get shit done, that's how to get it done, good job."

CHAPTER THIRTYTWO

It would be during this time period, that Eileen Sr would suddenly, for no apparent reason, end her relationship with Gil. Gil's previous wife actually worked and made a house payment or two and made sure she would get her hard earned share of the property's value. There was no way Eileen could get her name on the title deed to Gil's house. She tried, but failed, so for her it was time to move on.

Eileen Sr would now enter into a relationship that wasn't about money. Up until this relationship, EVERY single person she ever met, was viewed as a potential target. She cares nothing for ANY other human being on the planet. To Eileen Smith Sr, everyone is a possible source of income to support her completely out of control, downright disgusting slot machine habit.

Not this time though, this time it was about the sex. This guy was 20+ years younger than Eileen and dirt poor. Sex was so good, Eileen would support this young studs cocaine habit, money earmarked for her one and only true love, slot machines.

William didn't visit his mother very much these days, he didn't see eye to eye with his mothers new young boyfriend, he actually had to send this crackhead to the hospital to replace three teeth, and wire his jaw shut, after he was caught stealing from Eileen. The relationship ended less than a week later.

William had a lot of different things going on in his life at this time, he recently had gone thru a divorce, was estranged from his family, problems with his new career choice, AND, was sued for child support by his sons mother. The pressures and stress from all of this drama was building in side William, and soon would come the crescendo, the proverbial straw that broke the camels back.

Wednesday, November 23rd 2005, 9:45 pm, Thanksgiving eve. William and his assistant Steven, were still on the job site, finishing a home site that was going to have a Friday after thanksgiving walk thru with the home owner. The appliance's were in the living room, still needing to be installed, plus 6 or 7 pieces of tile were to be set and grouted, and some touch up paint throughout. Nothing William and Steven couldn't handle. Steven Garcia was the best partner William had ever had

Williams boss, Jim, was known to be the sneaky type when it came to checking on upcoming buyer walk-thru's, and at 9:45 walked in to this house William was working on, and proceeds to give William the riot act. William defended himself by the fact that he is there to finish all the work himself, even if it took all night. Jim wouldn't let up, as if William had said nothing at all. He kept screaming at William to the point that spittle was flying out of his mouth, and when a speck of that spittle hit William right in the eye, he turned away from Jim and told Steven calmly, "pack your tools, were going home."

Steven said, "but were not done."

"I don't care, if anything, we can finish tomorrow, before it's time for turkey" and even as William pulled away from the house, Jim was still screaming.

At the start of the long drive home, William slowed down where the highway crosses Peoples ditch, and chucked his company phone in it, and never went back, quit right then and there, didn't even bother to tell anyone he quit.

Less than 7 days later, William was notified that there was a check waiting for him at the main office. Severance pay they called it, but it was really 4 years of vacation pay William had accumulated, having never taken one during his tenure with the company.

William wanted something different, a change of venue, so to speak. Move away from this farming community that he has lived in for the past 15 years.

CHAPTER THIRTYTHREE

Eileen wasted no time finding her next potential victim, a man she met online, on one of those dating sites for senior's. His name was Brad and his bio on the web site stated that he liked to travel, the outdoors, and gambling. Eileen specifically chose this man because he had several serious health issues, with the hope that she would easily outlive him. As the relationship progressed, Eileen found out that he owned a valuable piece of real estate in the northern California town where he resided. She quickly gained his trust, and moved in with him, within weeks of meeting him.

William was already aware about his mothers new man, and had heard from Leslie that Brad owned some peach orchards, and that their sister Eileen Jr was already living with Eileen and <u>Brad</u>, and was supposed to be <u>helping</u> out with the orchard.

So William decided to call his mother to see how things were going at this man's farm. He wanted to see if there might be some work on Brads farm for him. It would be a good way for William to relocate, move away from all the bad memories associated with this farming community.

As it turned out, There was another relative, Williams nephew Jack was also living on the farm, working in the orchard. So when William spoke with his mother, she informed William that his nephew was not doing what he was supposed to be doing, actually, Jack was stealing from his grandmother. Eileen then asked William if he would be interested in coming to live on the farm, in exchange for some help straightening out this nephew, and making sure that Jack and Eileen Jr had done everything that needed to be done in the orchard.

William took his mother up on the offer, and relocated to this northern Californian town, where Brads peach orchard sits.

Upon arriving, one of the first things Eileen Sr mentioned to her son was that her laptop had recently gone missing, and that if he could please keep an eye out for it.

William got right to it, starting with the orchard. And, of course, there was a considerable amount of work to be done. Next up, the nephew, William decided that he would take Jack under his wing, try and teach him some responsibility. William figured the best way to accomplish this would be to find a job outside of the farm, something in construction. That way, William could use his vast amount of experience to show Jack that hard work pays off.

Within a week, William had found exactly the kind of work he was looking for, and began taking Jack to work with him. William did exactly what his mother asked of him, to the letter. But for some reason, she wasn't satisfied. And Jack seemed to be getting worse, not better. Every time Jack did something wrong, somehow it was now Williams fault. Every time Jack did something wrong, William was to blame, based on imaginary events, instead of what really happened.

And it was these very same lies, that would cause friction between William and Brad. It seemed like Eileen Jr and Jack were working together to make it look like William was the one stealing from the property. Eileen Sr did well to side with Jack and Eileen Jr's accusations. William was confused, how could his mother ask him for help, then turn on him like she did? Can you imagine how William felt?, coming to his mothers aide, just to get shit on?

It was all part of her scheme, just like his father before him, Eileen Sr wanted people that knew the family to see William like he was this great big giant piece of shit, which is absolutely not true. William loves his family with every fiber of his being. He would jump at any opportunity to help out one of his brothers or sisters.

William ended up getting into a big argument with Brad, and was asked to leave, which didn't really bother William all that much, especially the way his family was working against him.

3 days later, William was right back were he started, in central California, filled with despair. William then made one of the most profound decisions of his life. William made a conscious decision to just drop out of mainstream society, didn't want anything to do with "keeping up with the jones" anymore. Fuck working, fuck paying bills, forget all that shit, and all the bullshit requirements society puts on the masses.

Just look how it turned out for his father, Charles. His father went above and beyond the call of duty trying to please Eileen Sr. Just to be betrayed in the worst way possible. Aside from the 2 years William lived with his father in 89' and 90', Charles lived in that house alone, for the rest of his life.

CHAPTER THIRTYFOUR

William was now entering a very dark period in his life. He chose the red light district of this hick town to do what he called "chasing skirt".

But he was in complete denial about what he was really doing. He was diving head first into a world of pimps and prostitutes, drug dealers and drug addicts, rapist and murderers. It's hard to imagine, but eventually, there will be a silver lining to this time William spent running amuck on the streets.

And throughout these dark years, Leslie always took the time to seek out her little brother, especially each time she changed residences, recruiting William to help with the move. She would also allow William the luxury of staying over once in a while, mostly to help out with Leslie's grandkids, knowing they were safe in his care.

There was another reason Leslie kept tabs on her brother, it was something she was ordered to do by her mother, Eileen Sr.

You see, Eileen Sr tried in vain to have her name put on the title to Brads property. Was criticized by other members of Brads family concerning her attempt to gain a share of the farms equity.

A few years before this time, her husband Charles had quit smoking and drinking, causing his health to improve immensely, dashing her hopes that he would die before her. Her time to complete her evil plot was running short. She would soon step up her efforts.

Meanwhile, William was in a complete downward spiral, his drug use became an everyday occurrence. He started to become a hardcore addict.

The only thing that William would like to share about his 20+ year relationship with meth is this, methamphetamine is very much a double edged sword. Some narcotics affect the mind, most narcotics affect the body, but meth, it SERIOUSLY affects both the body and mind, SIMULTANEOUSLY, causing twice the damage to a user, than most other drugs. Truly a menace to society.

Throughout these dark years in William's life, he ended up in some pretty dangerous situations, by his own doing, no less. But then something happened that was completely out of his controlled.

June 14th, 2007, William had been living on his friend Carl's grandmothers property just a couple of miles out side of town. William got along well with Carl, helping out whenever something on the 3 acre property needed to be done. On this day in particular, the septic system wasn't working properly, causing the toilets to back up.

After spending the better part of an afternoon digging up leach lines, trying to resolve the problem, Carl told William to take a break, and that he was going to call a family friend named Nate to come and help them find the problem.

Nate was easily able to figure out that it would take replacing the entire septic tank. Although these systems seem worry free, that is an illusion, they do require a certain amount of maintenance.

Replacing the septic tank was beyond Carl and William's skill set, so it would have to be done professionally, leaving the property without a working toilet.

Nate is the kind of person that is the epitome, the very definition of the "give the shirt off his back to help a complete stranger" attitude towards his fellow man. Nate offered up a temporary solution to there situation. He was in possession of a portable toilet, stored on his property that was about 40 miles away. Nate was driving a old 59' Ford 3 ton flat bed work truck. The cab was so big, you could easily fit 4 people, plus the driver, steering wheel the size of a hoopla hoop.

Even though Nate and Carl could easily handle loading the outhouse onto the flat bed, Carl asked William if he wanted to go along for the ride. Tired from digging all afternoon, William declined the offer. Carl was fine with that, But right before they got in the truck to leave, Nate offered to buy William dinner at a popular hole in the wall called The Chuck Wagon, famous for their foot long chili dogs.

There are 3 things in this life that William has absolutely NEVER said NO to......

WORK

A DECENT MEAL

And

WOMEN

Period.

William was not about to miss out on one of those chili dogs, and agreed to go. As they traveled the 2 lane country road on their way to Nate's property, the chatter was constant. Shortly after leaving one of the many intersections, there was a mid sized, black sedan travelling towards them in the other direction. When these two vehicles were about a hundred yards apart, the driver of the black sedan dropped his 24 oz can of beer and then reached down in an effort to save his beloved courage in a can, causing him to cross the double yellow line, right in front of Nate's truck, hitting them head on at a combined speed of 110 mph. The impact is so catatonic that both the driver, Nate, and passenger, Carl are ejected instantly. William, who was sitting middle, without a seat belt, is bounced around like a pinball in a pinball machine, as this 3 ton monster goes airborne, does a half flip, and lands on the roof of the cab. William was upside down, with his feet on that very same roof. As the truck slid to a stop, the cab collapsed, literally crushing William, and trapping him inside for the most terrifying 12 minutes of his life.

Carl was thrown 400 feet down the road, and with a moderate injury to his back, got up off the pavement and ran back to the wreck in an effort to free William. His attempt was futile, the truck was upside down, cab supports had crushed inwards, almost impaling William. All Carl could do was reach in through a small opening and place his hand on William's leg, trying to comfort him, telling him help is on the way.

William screamed, "where's Nate!?, go see if he is ok, maybe he can help you get me out of here, hurry!!!"

"I think he went to get help, he took off running down the street." Carl said.

William panicked, he actually thought Nate might have abandoned ship.

Even though Nate was ejected, on impact he tightened his grip on the steering wheel, causing his legs to go out the window first and as the vehicle rotated, he slid out of the window, landing on his feet, unharmed. When he saw the cab collapse, he bolted. He ran to a nearby business and came back to the wreck riding on the back of a FORKLIFT ! And with that equipment's help, lifted that truck up off the ground enough to pry off the roof and free William from the wreckage, very possibly saving William's life.

By God's grace, everyone survived, but both William and the driver of the sedan were seriously injured. The driver of the sedan actually had a crescent shaped piece of his body missing from the impact causing the steering wheel to go right through the side of his chest, missed his heart by a couple of inches.

William had his left arm permanently dislocated from his shoulder, fractured the right side of his hip in two places, and a serious concussion.

He was discharged from the hospital in a wheelchair, and would not regain the ability to walk for 3 months.

He desperately needed help from his family, but received not one bit of help from them. Eileen Sr even accused William of lying about the wreck, that he was trying to con her out of some money.

Never once did he ask her for money. No lady, your son was really almost killed, and really needed some help. He wasn't trying to con you out of your money for your precious slot machines. William's family just left him to suffer.

When Nate found about this, he jumped into action. He was not about to just leave William to suffer like that. Nate made sure William had a roof over his head, made sure he had stuff to eat, took William to all his doctor's appointments, and rehabilitation. Nate took care of everything, and was happy to do it.

Nate has more class in his little pinky, than Eileen Smith has in her whole entire Vicodin and nicotine polluted body.

The man is a real life superhero. May God truly bless him.

William's life would never be the same. Anyone that has ever survived a tragedy like this, knows the difficulty's that come with surviving a head on collision. For some survivors, there in an inescapable fear of even being a passenger in a car, let alone drive one.

William has never fully recovered, 100%, from this near death event. It was also the driving force that caused William to become permanently home-less for the next 15 years.

By coincidence, William's sister Leslie became homeless herself for a few of these years. It was during this time that both of these siblings would jump at the chance to help out one another. William felt that a bond was forming between his sister and himself. A level of trust unsurpassed out of any other members of the family.

CHAPTER THIRTYFIVE

Diane Turnberry.

Here comes the silver lining.

Up until William met Diane, he was still, after all these years, a very naïve person. But that was about to change drastically.

It's true what some people say about the difference between "book smarts" and "street smarts". Let's say the apocalypse happens, and society completely goes to shit. Most conformist and suburbanites, people with "book smarts", will not survive for very long.

People with "streets smarts", on the other hand, already have the skills needed to be able to survive the apocalypse.

William reached a turning point in his life when he met Diane. His relationship with her was like a crash course on how to stay safe living on the streets.

William met Diane through some mutual friends, a couple named Sherrie and Alicia. It was during a visit to the couple's home, Diane and her adult daughter, Megan were visiting also.

As the evening was winding down, Diane asked William if he would walk with Megan to her next destination. The neighborhood was notoriously dangerous, and William agreed to escort Megan to one of her friends houses, that was about 3 blocks away. And that's exactly what William did, to the letter. And that was that, or so William thought.

A week later, William bumped into Sherrie at a local liquor store. Sherrie told William that Diane really liked him and wanted to know if he wanted to hook up. William told Sherrie to tell her friend that he's not looking to hook up with anyone at the moment.

But just days later, William bumped into Alicia at the same liquor store, and she went on to tell William how Diane really liked him and wanted hook up with him, even if it was just a one night stand.

William asked Alicia, "that's all she wants, some sex???"

Alicia said, "that's what she said".

William told Alicia, "ok, let me talk to this woman, tell her to meet me at the park tonight."

The conversation ended with Alicia, "ok, I'll tell her."

Later that evening, William met with Diane at the old oak tree.

After some small talk, William wanted Diane to fully understand how he felt about her and what they were about to do.

William said, "ok, Diane, I'll do this with you tonight, but don't be surprised tomorrow if I act like I don't even know you. I'm not trying to be mean or anything, it's just that I'm not doing the relationship thing out here on the streets like this. Ok? Are you going to be ok with that?"

"Yeah, I think I can handle that" was her response.

The deed was done, the act itself didn't have the level of passion to justify a second encounter. At least that's how William felt about it

Diane, on the other hand, wanted more. Even though she agreed to a one night stand, the very next day, Diane came to William with the "when can we see each other again?" routine.

William did his best to ward off her advances, but Diane was very persistent, literally courting William. She would always show up, unannounced, at all different hours of the day. And Diane ALWAYS had something for William when she came to visit him, food, money, clothes, whatever she thought William might need.

For 6 months Diane tried to get William into a committed relationship. And even though he knew better, her persistence paid off, and William agreed to give it a go with this woman.

Diane was very street wise, and began to peel away the layers of innocence that have surrounded William his whole life.

She taught him how to read a person's body language, how to pay better attention to everything that was going on around him. She even patiently taught him how to see himself through other people's eyes, making it possible for William take notice when someone is getting ready to victimize him.

She also taught him that sometimes, foul people will literally tell on themselves, before, during, or after they do something foul.

But like most relationship's that start in less than ideal conditions, this relationship was full of problems. It had it's ups and downs, and they would separate for months at a time, and then try and start all over again. Some times when they were broken up, Diane liked to show up at like 3 or 4 in the morning, trying to catch William in bed with another woman.

CHAPTER THIRTYSIX

William had been running amuck on the streets, ripping and tearing for close to ten years by now, in 2013, and has earned his stripes, so to speak.

But believe it or not, he never really victimized anyone. William was called upon when some one was being bullied, or robbed, or being taken advantage of. On several occasions, William kicked in someone's door to rescue people or property.

It was during that summer that William started using some of the knowledge He had recently obtained to help keep his girlfriend safe. It all started one day when Diane informed William that she thought she was being followed by some big Indian guy while he was at work. For the next couple of days, William searched the neighborhood for this guy to see what he was about. When William finally did spot this big Indian guy, William was about a quarter mile or so away from his camp and watched this Indian guy enter his camp. William immediately went to go see what this guy was doing in his camp. When William finally made it to his camp, the Indian guy was nowhere in sight. Nothing in the camp was disturbed, there were several valuable items left untouched. That left William confused as to what he was doing in his camp, what was this Indian guy looking for?

The next day, William had to go out of town for a couple of days, and when he returned, Diane told him that the Indian guy was following her around the whole time. She was so scared that she decided to stay with some friends, instead of staying at their camp.

William wanted to know what was going on with this Indian guy and searched the whole neighborhood for him, without any luck. Diane and William called it a day, and went to their camp for the night.

The next morning, a friend of Williams that lived in the same vicinity, told William, "hey, I was in and out a lot last night, and there was this Indian guy hiding in the bushes, it looked like he was watching your spot or something, I asked him what he was doing and he told me he was waiting for his girlfriend, but nobody ever showed up, and I thought you should know about it."

William answered, "thanks Justin, I appreciate you letting me know, I've been having an issue with this guy, and now I know he's stalking my girl, wait 'til I find this fool".

It now made sense to William why nothing was messed with the day this Indian was in Williams camp. He wasn't looking for something, he was looking for someone, he was looking for Diane.

After Justin left Williams camp, William told Diane, "As soon as you see that guy, you come get me as fast as you can, I will solve this problem right now". And that's exactly what William did.

Two days later, Diane returned from the grocery store and told William "babe, I saw that guy over by Labor Ready."

Labor Ready is a little over a quarter mile away from the park that William and Diane camp at, just off the main boulevard, on a side street.

Upon hearing the news, William immediately strapped on his shoes, then took off running on his way to confront this Indian guy. When William got to the boulevard, he started running faster on the left side of the street, against traffic. When he got to the side street, he finally spotted this Indian guy. Without looking for traffic, William crossed the boulevard and ran up to this Indian guy saying "who the fuck do you think you are, stalking my girl?"

William didn't wait for an answer, and put his fist squarely on this idiots chin, knocking this Indian guy on his ass, nearly knocked him out. Then William stood over this Indian guy and was about to explain to him why he shouldn't stalk other people's girlfriends, without using words.

That's when the police officer that shadowed William ever since William started running down the boulevard, decided to intervene.

Just as William raised his fist to start pounding on this predator, the cop said, "you just hold on a minute there, sir!"

The officer got out of his patrol car and told William, "sit your ass down and let me see some ID!"

William sat down and got his drivers license out and gave it to the officer. As he did so, the Indian guy got up off the ground and quickly started walking away, leaving the bags he was carrying behind.

The cop asked William, "why is my victim leaving the scene?"

"I don't know." Was Williams answer.

"You stay right there, mister!" and the officer got back into his patrol car to go catch up with this Indian guy and find out why he split.

He caught up with him about 100 yards away and got out of his patrol car to talk to him. About 4 minutes later, the cop slapped some handcuffs on this guy and put him in the back of his car.

William figured that he better go get his license, and approached the officer and said, "officer, can I get my license back?"

What this cop said next, blew Williams mind, the cop said, "Mr. Smith, is there anything else I can do for you today?" as he held out Williams license.

William snatched it out of his hand saying, "nope, I'm good, you have a nice day officer."

For all rights and intentions, William should of went to jail that day, the cop was witness to an assault. But the guy that got assaulted is the one who went to jail. Why?

The answer is simple. Right before William punched Indian guy in the face, the cop heard William say something about stalking, and when the cop ran this Indian guy's name, found out that Indian guy was on parole, after being released from prison for raping women, and the stalking accusation would easily revoke his parole and send him back to prison. Good job William, helping get this violent criminal off the streets.

William would later find out exactly what this Indian guy was all about from his friend Mike. Turns out that Indian guy likes to slip girls a "mickey" a drug to get them to pass out, and then he would rape them. Indian guy tried to victimize Mikes girl, but she was able to fight him off.

Good thing for that Indian guy the cops got to him before Mike did, because what Mike was going to do to him, was much, much worse than the beating William wanted to give him.

Let's just say that the hole that the Indian guy was going to be put in, was already dug.

Not long after William dealt with that big Indian guy, Diane and William got into one of their biggest arguments to date, and would go their separate ways for the next several months.

CHAPTER THIRTYSEVEN

Ever since William returned from New York, almost 20 years ago, he only talked to his father a handful of times. But in December of 2013, Leslie's new husband, "Pops", for some reason asked William if he had talked to his father lately, which by the way, William hadn't. Pops suggested that he do so, telling William that he had heard from Eileen Sr that his health was starting to go bad, and that he should talk to him before it's too late.

This puzzled William because the last time William called his dad, Charles was very up beat about life, and how quitting smoking and drinking has made him feel better than he has felt in years. William was determined to find out just what has changed and wasted no time in giving his father a call.

The call was not much different than the half dozen or so that came before it. No sudden on set of illness, no accident to cause some injury, his father was as healthy as he's ever been. Although, he was excited about the new television He ordered on line, for his bedroom, finally arriving. His excitement was from the new technology this electronic device came equipped with. It had a built in VCR and Blu-ray player built right into the TV, so he could enjoy his favorite movies and programs from the comfort of his bed. Charles was very adamant about never falling asleep in the living room.

William didn't understand why Pops would tell him his dad was sick, when he wasn't, and actually Charles health was improving. But the call was good and put Williams worries to rest. William never bothered to ask Pops where he got his info, all that really mattered was that his dad was ok.

William made sure not to burden his sister Leslie and her new husband with his needs, and kept his visits to once a month or so.

The very next time William went to visit Leslie and Pops, he didn't get an answer the first time he knocked. William decided it might be to early(8:15 am), and left to run an errand, returning about 45 minutes later. This time when he knocked, some person William had never seen before answered the door. William immediately went inside and demanded to see his sister and her husband. That's when this unknown person told William that both his sister and Pops were in the hospital.

William didn't even notice the man and woman that were sitting on the living room couch when he left to go to the hospital and find out what happened and why they were both in the hospital.

Pops condition was so severe, William was unable to visit him, his sister's condition was not much better. When he got to her room, his emotions got the best of him, and he started to cry as he asked her what happened.

Leslie told her brother, "little brother, I appreciate that your worried about me, but I need you to go back to our apartment, get my phone, get my keys, and get those people out of my house, please, I mean right now!"

William said, "ok sis." And headed back to the apartment. William now had a name for this guy that answered his sister's door. William didn't bother knocking this time, he just went in and told Steve, "I want the keys and my sister's phone right now, and then you people are going to leave right now."

That's when William noticed the couple sitting on the couch.

Steve handed William his sister's phone, and said he had to retrieve the keys from the back room.

That's when William decides to do a walk thru to make sure nothing is missing. Pops guitars and drum set, check. All the electronics, check. His sister's bedroom looks in order, so he returned to the living room to get the keys from Steve and clear everyone out and get back to the hospital.

But Steve was nowhere in sight. The couple sitting on the couch told William that Steve left to go use the phone, but William had a working phone in his hand, what gives?

William then told this couple, "your not going to disrespect me for one more second, now get your shit and get out!" as they gathered their stuff the woman started crying. And they didn't exactly leave the property either, they went and sat on the curb out front, possibly waiting for Steve to return. Steve was gone for so long that William was able to clean a kitchen that looked like a grenade had been thrown in the sink.

Steve finally returned telling his two friends, "yeah, guys, we got to go" and finally gave William the keys. William wouldn't even let Steve back in the apartment, locked everything up, and went straight back to the hospital.

It was the weirdest thing, as Steve followed behind William, staying a considerable distance away from him on their way back to the hospital.

William made it to his sister's room first, Steve entered the room seconds later. Steve went straight over to Leslie and whispered something in her ear.

"They want to know if they can stay one more night so they can take showers and stuff", Leslie told her brother.

William responded with, "hell no, I don't even want to be there without you guys there!"

Leslie told her brother, " but I need you to go back to our apartment and check on some stuff Andrea has stored in the garage".

That's when Steve just up and left, didn't say goodbye, or hope you get better or anything like that. Just left without saying a word to anyone.

Leslie's friend Andrea had stored two jet skis and a motor cycle in the garage.

When William tried to get in the garage, he was unsuccessful. None of the keys on his sister's keyring fit ANY of the locks on the garage. William was at a loss.

Leslie told William to do whatever it takes to get in that garage. So William borrowed some bolt cutters and cut the lock off the garage door. Two jet skis, check. A motorcycle, check.

William let Leslie know that everything was there, and that he was on his way back. But Leslie wanted him to stay at the garage, because Andrea wanted to come and get the skis and motorcycle.

When Andrea arrived, the first thing she said was, "hey William, where's the motorcycle ramp?"

"what motorcycle ramp?" he said.

The ramp for the motorcycle was not in the garage like it was supposed to be. They couldn't find it anywhere.

That made it very difficult to get the motorcycle loaded onto Andrea's truck, but they managed to get it done. Andrea was pretty upset over the missing ramp, and the only people that would know, would be the people that were there, Steve and his friends, and they were long gone.

Andrea chalked it up as a loss, and then thanked William for all the help. Right as she was getting ready to leave, Andrea got a call from Leslie, asking to have William let her in to the apartment so Andrea could retrieve a personal item for Leslie.

While William waited in the living room, he tried to turn on the TV, but it wouldn't turn on. When William looked behind the entertainment center, he found that ALL the electronics had been disconnected and the cords had all been wound up, like when a person is preparing to move.

William was starting to think that maybe this guy Steve was up to no good during the week him and his friends were in the apartment.

It was a couple of weeks later, after Pops was released from the hospital, that the mystery about the motorcycle ramp would be solved.

Pops found out that the night before William showed up, his neighbor was doing some late night yard work, because the weather was too hot to do it during the day. And the neighbor told Pops that he witnessed Steve put what looked like a motorcycle ramp in the back of a green pick up.

It now made sense to William why all the electronics were unhooked. Steve and his friends were in the process of clearing out Pops and Leslie's apartment.

If William had waited just one more day to have his once a month visit, Steve and company would have stolen everything they owned, including Andrea's motorcycle and jet skis.

Sometimes, timing really is everything.

CHAPTER THIRTYEIGHT

ERE WE GO
June, 2014, it was just weeks after Leslie was released from the hospital that she gave William some very bad news. She informed her brother that their father, Charles had died.

And of course William wanted to know when, how, and why. Leslie told her brother that he died April 8th of that same year. William briefly wondered why she waited two whole months to tell him. She also stated that he died in his sleep one night from an enlarged heart and that he FELL ASLEEP ON THE LIVING ROOM COUCH, and wasn't discovered for several days. She also added that he had a two space heaters facing him. But wait a minute, it was unseasonably warm during the month of April that year. Unfortunately, William didn't have much time to give any of this information much thought.

The very next thing out of Leslie's mouth was that his dad had a mesothelioma fund and that all of his children were required to sign a release from in order to receive some money.

To William, what his sister was telling him was just believable enough that he agreed to sign this release from. Add in the enormous amount of trust that William thought there was between his sister and himself, he assumed everything was legit, on the up and up.

The day it was time to go sign this paper, Leslie was uncharacteristically generous with her weed that particular morning, making sure William was good and intoxicated. William was so high that he didn't really read what he was signing, not to mention, he didn't notice that both Leslie and her daughter Helen signed the paper also.

A week or so later, Eileen Sr came to Leslie and Pops house to give William some money. 8000 dollars to be exact. And life was just peachy keen for William. He was single at the time and it only took a few weeks for William to spend the bulk of the 8000 grand his mother gave him.

Around this same time, unexpected and out of the blue, Williams older brother, Ted, contacted William and told his little brother that he was leaving his wife that he had been married to for the last 20 years and needed help relocating. William told Ted that he was living in a tent at the park, but he would try and help him anyway he could.

Ted would start visiting William a couple of times a week, and the third time Ted came to see William, Ted was adamant about seeing exactly where Williams camp was located. Even though William gave his older brother easy to follow directions, Ted wouldn't leave it at that, he insisted that William physically show him where his camp was, and William did.

The last part of their conversation was Ted asking William, "so, you stay here alone? Nobody else stays here with you?"

William answered, "yup, all by myself. It's been over between me and Diane for awhile now, and I'm not seeing anyone at the moment, so I'll be by myself, at least for the near future"

Ted said, "that has to suck, right?"

William, "It's not that bad, I don't mind."

Then Ted ended the conversation saying, "well, I have to go now, I have some people waiting for me, maybe I'll come and see you tomorrow."

"Ok, by." William was glad his big brother wanted to be in his life now, it made William feel good about himself.

EARLY the next morning, around 3:45 am, Diane showed up at Williams camp, unannounced, trying to talk William into getting back together. It all ways upset William when Diane woke him up so early like this, and Diane would offer to buy breakfast at a local diner, known for having excellent food. The diner opened good and early, at 5 am, and it was about 4:50 when they left camp to go eat.

As they were leaving, William noticed a man he didn't recognize at first, standing next to a tree that was just off the path that led to Williams camp. The man had something shiny in his hand and Diane could tell by the way he was holding it, that it was a gun. A 45 caliber hand gun to be exact.

Diane said, "babe, he's got a gun."

William, has never had any known enemies his whole life, and didn't think he was here to harm them. William assumed that maybe they just interrupted someone getting ready to commit suicide.

"He's not here for us, let's hurry up", William told Diane.

As they walked past this guy, William made sure he was in between this gunman and his girlfriend. And you could bet, William kept a close eye on this guy as they walked past him.

Right as William was as close as he was going to get to this guy, BRIAN SMITH told William, who didn't recognize that it was his little brother, "DON'T LOOK AT ME!!!"

So William turned away from him, and hurried on his way.

When William felt they were out of earshot, he said to Diane, "I think that guy is here to kill himself."

Diane corrected William, saying, " no babe, he's here to hurt someone"

It went back and forth, off himself, hurt someone, off himself, hurt someone. Then William said to Diane, " that looked like it could have been my little brother."

"you haven't spoken to him in almost 30 years, why would he show up here with his gun?" she asked.

William said, " he doesn't know where I live, (William didn't know it, but there was a reason Ted was so adamant about knowing exactly where his camp was the night before) maybe it just happened to be where he decided to go to whack himself. I don't know."

Diane added, "are you 100% sure that was him?"

"No, not even close" with that said, William didn't bother to think about what he just saw anymore.

And William didn't even notice that Ted, not only didn't come to visit like he said he would, he stopped visiting altogether.

Brian Smith had just failed his mother, Eileen Smith Sr, in a big way.

On Williams next visit to Leslie's, she didn't seem very happy to see him. She sounded annoyed every time William said something, like hearing her brothers voice caused her some kind of pain and anguish.

Over the next few weeks, William noticed that other people at his sister's were acting strange as well.

Pops, for example, would come out of pocket every time William came through their door. He would just, for no apparent reason, give William some money, or some weed, packs of cigarettes, even expensive gadgets.

William couldn't figure out why Pops was doing this, but decided to not push the issue.

Then, out of nowhere, Leslie started to accuse William of stealing from her. Completely not true. 35 years ago, William stole an eighth of pot from Leslie's husband, and that was the only time he even came close to stealing from one of his other siblings. The very idea of stealing from his family never even entered his mind. What gives???

CHAPTER THIRTYNINE

It wasn't long before William ran into his brother, Ted. William wanted to know why he stopped visiting, but instead of answering Williams questions, Ted said something totally bizarre, like they weren't even having the same conversation.

"You know William, I'm all for you getting your inheritance back."

What the fuck!, what inheritance, nobody ever told me about no inheritance, William thought to himself.

Ted went on to say, "yeah, they got you good, and there's nothing you can do about it."

William came back with, "Why, because I signed that paper?"

"Yeah, something like that."

William had all kinds of questions, but Ted didn't have much to say after that, only that, "you sure got the shortest end of your mother's stick."

William started to really worry about what the fuck was going on. William had two questions that he desperately wanted answered.

#1 What exactly was this paper he signed?

AND,

#2 Why the fuck was his little brother at his camp with a gun in his hand?

4 different times, William asked Leslie what exactly was this paper he signed and got 4 completely different answers.

William tried desperately to obtain a copy of this paper he signed, but didn't even know where to start. He didn't even know what kind of document it was. Without knowing what he signed, made it virtually impossible for him to contest it.

More than just the paper he signed, William desperately tried to contact his little brother and ask him what exactly he was doing at his camp with a gun in his hand. William used every social media platform he could think of, Facebook, Twitter, messenger, and even paid for the premium service on Likenden and got no response. And by using those services, it guarantee's that Brian's devices received all the messages William sent, and he knows exactly how his older brother feels.

William also went to great lengths to find out if he really did inherit something when his father died. He told his story to dozens of lawyers and law firms and got no where. William even went to the Bar Association, only to be told by one of their lawyers that all of his answers are in New York.

Next, William focused his thoughts on the notary public where this paper signing took place. William was so high that day, he didn't really remember where this notary's office was located.

It is a personal belief of this author that every single nano second of our lives is stored in our brains, just like a computers memory bank. But for people in every day life, we don't have the capacity to retrieve a particular moment in our past at will. The information is there, but we don't have access to it like a computer.

William racked his mind for days trying to remember where this notary was, and it was driving him crazy.

Then, all of the sudden one day it came to him in a flash, right in front of his eyes. He now remembered right where the notary was located.

He wasted no time going to see this notary to find out exactly what he signed. Unfortunately, because William couldn't remember the title of the document, and the exact date that he signed it, the notary was unable to give William the information he was seeking.

All the while, William had no idea what his family was trying to do to him, probably because what they were trying to do was un-imaginable, un-fathomable, and down right evil.

Completely oblivious to the very real danger he was in.

Even though William wasn't exactly sure WHAT it was his "didn't even pretend to be" mother was in the process of stealing, but he was 100% sure it was SOMETHING. And William wanted to let this person (William used that term like it was a feather) know how he felt about her. Told her that "gold digging whores are a better class of people than you!!!" and was responded to with a dial tone, typical of someone that just heard the truth about themselves.

And just minutes after that phone call ended, William got a call from Eileen Jr, of all people, and she then proceeded to threaten William with bodily harm by saying "you better stop harassing mom for money, or I'll send some of my scary biker friends to fuck you up!" those were her exact words.

William absolutely NEVER asked his mother (again, like a feather) for money, at least not in the past 15 or maybe even 20 years, so he screamed back at his sister "this ain't got anything to do with motherfucking money!!!"

Two things were about to happen,

First, upon hearing her brother spit out a truth about himself, (William has never been about money, and Eileen Jr knows that good and well) Eileen Jr's brain switched to subconscious mode.

And second, Eileen Jr would say something to William that would make him realize that he really was in danger.

The next thing she said to her brother was, "Oh yeah, it's not about money, right little brother, then how come when dad died the basement had hundreds of expensive power tools in it, and how come he turned your room into a state of the art, architecture room, with computers and a fancy drafting board, how about that, huh little brother?"

Without having to think too much about what she just said, William asked, "how the fuck do you know what the house looked like and what was in it when he died??? Were you in New York when he died???"

Her answer to that was, "you know what asshole?, I don't have to tell you anything, FUCK YOU!" and hung up.

Eileen Jr had just literally told on herself, forgot who she was talking too, admitted to William that she was indeed, in the house either before, during, or right after he died, possibly all three. And very possibly involved in his death, in some way.

William, About 8 minutes later, called the FBI, To voice his concern that he believed that there was some kind foul play concerning his father's death, at the hands of his mother. The agent William spoke with, told him that the information he was providing didn't have enough "investigative value" to warrant using their "limited resources" to start any kind of investigation. Then this FBI agent decided to LIE to William, telling William that they could only investigate the verbal threat and then did absolutely nothing, no person to contact, no follow up, nothing, like William never talked to them at all.

When Eileen Sr found out what her daughter, Eileen Jr, had told William about her being in New York, everyone in William's family that was involved was ordered to stop any and all communication with William. Eileen Sr was extremely upset with Eileen Jr, going as far as threatening her life in retaliation for giving William such damming information.

William was determined to find out the truth about what he signed, find out the truth about why his little brother confronted him with a gun in his hand. William would seek solitude, and move his camp to a spot behind the old cemetery, in an effort to intensely search his memory, as far back as he could remember.

William made it a point, when visiting this cemetery, to stop and pay his respects to a man named Clovis M. Cole. Williams admiration for this man stems from this man's accomplishments during his 96 years of life. It starts with his headstone, which reads, "HERE LIES CLOVIS M. COLE, FOUND-ER OF THE CITY OF CLOVIS CALIFORNIA! May he rest in peace."

Quite the accomplishment to attain even once in a lifetime, to have created a city right out of the bare dirt. But, ladies and gentlemen, it was his THIRD TIME reaching that mile stone! Clovis, New Mexico, and Clovis, Texas both proudly wear his name. He created 3 great American cities, with his bare hands. He was undoubtedly, one truly amazing person.

CHAPTER FORTY

Most of the day and a half William spent in solitude, literally searching his memory, was physically done so with his eyes closed. But in reality, the eyes of Williams mind were now wide open, and every bit of credit goes to his girlfriend, Diane. If it had not been for this woman's unwavering, truly authentic, and deeply profound love for William, he would have never learned so many important things about how foul, and evil people from ANY genre, really are.

And as he searched his memory, starting with the present, and working backwards, all the way back to his childhood, his earliest memories. And to help him remember things he might have missed, started again, working from childhood going forward. Sifting through 45 years of madness.

His effort was not in vain, he remembered a lot of things long forgotten, conversations he had with Eileen seniors sister, Williams aunt Barbara. Things he over heard his dad say to his friends. Most recently, and importantly, things like how his niece Helen's husband David, died suddenly in the hospital, not long after Brian Smith tried to murder William, and while David was being treated for some fractured ribs, not broken, routine shit. The hospital somehow collapsed both his lungs, put him on life support, and less than a week later, Someone in David's family told the hospital to pull the plug. WHY???

Maybe it was because David, being Helen Eileen Smith's former husband, had wondered why Helen's last name was Smith and figured out for himself the horrifying reason this person is named, basically, Eileen Smith. The threat of David possibly sharing that information with any one, justification for silencing him permanently.

William also remembered how his older brother Ted was behaving the night before little brother made his attempt to end Williams life. William had a profound realization, if Diane had not shown up that fateful morning, his brother Brian would have surely put a bullet in his head. Ted most assuredly reported that William would be alone. William firmly believes it was the hand of God that placed Diane with him that day, literally saving Williams life.

It was at that moment, after he finished with his memories, he came to the horrifying conclusion that his family was trying to murder him. ALL OF THEM!!! We are talking all 4 of his siblings, people William truly <u>LOVES</u> with every fiber of his being, people he believed were in the same fight, same struggle that life is, people he was downright GOOD to, trying desperately to end their brothers INNOCENT life.

William now embarked on a somewhat intense investigation of his own, and decided to rattle the notary's cage, force the notary to do the right thing, and help William obtain any information about this document that nearly cost him his life. William began to literally terrorize the notary, right at his office, and in front of his other customers. William would just walk right in and accuse the notary of being involved in this plot to murder him, and tell his customers what a big giant piece of shit this notary is. This harassment lasted almost 3 weeks, at which point William felt defeated.

Less than a week later, William was walking past the notary's office, minding his own business, when the notary came running out of his office, yelling "hey William, hey William, I remember you now, I have something for you."

The notary handed William his ledger from the day William signed this paper, and it contained a wealth of information.

On December 22nd, 2014 William unknowingly signed a "waiver of citation" giving Helen Eileen Smith power of attorney over his inheritance. This is not something William inherited from his father. This was something he inherited from his grandfather, "Charlie" Smith. It is very likely that whatever William inherited, was a birthright. And for whatever reason, the birthright skipped a generation. The only possible reason William won the birthright, is because his grandfather decreed that Charles first born son to have a son, and therefore carry on the family name, would inherit their grandfather's estate. And because Ted Smith never fathered any children, William was the first born son to have an heir.

Up until this moment, William didn't know that his niece, Helen, had the middle name <u>Eileen</u>, and the last name <u>Smith</u>. William thought to himself, "wait a minute, when Helen was born, Leslie was still married to James and Jack's father, making her legal name Danbury and the father's name was Goff, why the fuck did they name Helen, Eileen Smith!?!?"

CHAPTER FORTYONE

And now, so the world at large can fully understand exactly what Eileen Barnes (per Williams request, for the remainder of this tragic tale, Eileen WILL NOT be referred to as Eileen Smith. That person didn't even come within a hundred yards of the goal line that is the right to wear the Smith title, kind of like in the game of football when the team on offense (Eileen) gets tackled in their own end zone, and the defense (William) is awarded 2 points. In relation to this story, it's very ironic that, that play is called a "safety".

So let's sum up exactly what Eileen Barnes perpetrated throughout her life long career of murderous fraud.

Back in the late 1950's, Eileen Barnes was a lazy, hateful, waste of a human life, with absolutely no future in front of her. When she found out she had gotten pregnant by her brother, decided to target Charles Smith. She seduced this man once, then conned him into believing it was really his child, subsequently forcing his hand into marrying her. Then Eileen agreed to help Charles raise his little sister as their daughter. Eileen obtained the information concerning the birthright, and purposely withheld that information from Charles. She bore 3 sons, again purposely poisoning Ted and William in the womb, hoping to make them both sterile and retarded. (Succeeded with Ted, obviously failed with William).

Then in 1981, with the help of the 3 oldest Smith children, literally kidnapped William and Brian completely abandoning Charles for the last 37 years of Charles life, traveling 3200 miles to the other side of the country. During the first few years in California, Eileen tried to victimize an innocent man named Gilbert, but realized Gilbert's ex had already secured half of Gilbert net worth, and so abandoned that man as well. In 1989, Eileen victimized a grocery store, faking a slip and fall, and robbing this grocer of over 75,000 dollars. In 1994, Eileen Sr ORDERED Eileen Jr to drive to New York and murder one of Eileen Sr foster parents, Mrs. Uncino. Then sold the Uncino's 800,000 dollar mansion for less than 329,000 dollars, LITERALLY flushing a half a million dollars, right down the toilet that is her gambling habit. (Proving without a shadow of a doubt that Eileen Barnes has the I.Q. of a maggot) When William fathered his son Scott Smith, Eileen ORDERED Leslie to have a child asap, so they could name that child Eileen Smith. (Eileen Barnes, and Leslie Smith both committed a very real, very serious felony, called INFINTACIDE. (Attempted) its when a parent brings a child into the world, knowing before that child is born, that they are going to eventually murder that child.) Confused? Helen was talked into signing the waiver of citation with William, Eileen Smith, leaving out the Helen part of her name, Eileen Barnes did this so she could murder both William and Helen, then show this waiver of citation to the probate court and state that "look, he signed his inheritance over to me, Eileen Smith before he died!" 100%truth!!!

One of the most important parts of this plot for Eileen Barnes was never granting Charles a divorce, by never divorcing Charles, made Eileen Sr next of kin, according to the laws in the state of New York. So whatever William inherited from his fathers blood line, according to the state of New York, she legally takes possession of the inheritance AND IS NOT LEGALLY OBLIGATED TO TELL WILLIAM about it. And she didn't and denies to this day that William inherited anything.

When Brian Smith failed to murder his innocent brother, it made the waiver of citation a worthless piece of paper, might as well have been a piece of tissue that the nigger piece of shit Hitler used to wipe his nigger ass.

Brian's failed attempt would not end the danger William was in, William knows that there were at least 4 more attempts. Most recent, and noteworthy is an attempt that occurred just a few months before this second edition of this story was published in late 2021.

It happened in the very same spot as Brian's attempt. William was repairing his bicycle in the park one afternoon, and had just purchased a 64 oz. soda before he started. Out of nowhere, a youngster that just recently started living in William's neighborhood and that was not known by anyone in the neighborhood, approached William and told William that he had just got some RC cola and if William would like some. William picked up his still full, brand new 64 oz soda and shook it so this youngster would know it was full.

"No thanks, I just got me a soda already." William said.

About 10 minutes later, this youngster walked up to William and said, "here's that soda you wanted." And tried to hand William some RC soda that was in a very old 16oz clear glass Pepsi bottle, with a 805 beer bottle cap pressed on the top, AND IT WAS IN A BROWN PAPER BAG!!!

It's a mathematical certainty that this youngster nobody had ever seen before was trying to do something foul.

"Are you fucking blind, or just stupid, you know as well as I do, that I have an ice cold soda right here, why are you pushing the issue?" William said. The youngster couldn't give William an answer, he just put his down and mumbled something as he walked away. When a person can not explain their behavior, at the very least, that person is lying, and most likely up to no good.

CHAPTER FORTYTWO

Not many people that know William, and most of his closest friends, can ever come close to understanding exactly what William is going through. For close to 47 years of his life, William believed that his family actually loved him, just to find out one day that it was all a lie. To find out one day that ALL OF THEM, and I mean all of them, husbands, boyfriends, nieces, nephews, even family friends were all involved in the plot to murder William, someone that was good to all if them, and they were in it for financial gain of all things. THERE IS NOT ONE PERSON IN THIS WHOLE ENTIRE COMMUNITY, other than Williams family, THAT CAN LABEL WILLIAM A FOUL PER-SON!!! NOT EVEN CLOSE. Their was still a very tiny bit of doubt that what Ted said to William about "your inheritance" was even true. But soon, William would get definite confirmation(not from any legal organization, I will explain that in a later chapter) that he did indeed inherit something.

Right after Brian confronted William with his 45 cal. Gun in his hand, William's niece, Helen had found herself a new boyfriend, named Vick, who, by the way, had been recently released from prison after serving 9 years of a 10 year sentence for MANSLAUGHTER, which means he basically got away with murdering someone. The first time William met Vick, it was at Leslie and Pops house. When Vick walked in their house he immediately started doing something that is called "eye fucking" everything in the house. For those of you who don't know what that is, it's when someone evaluates everything they see inside someone's home, literally picking and choosing what they are going to eventually steal from that house. He didn't even try to hide the fact that he was casing all the items in Leslie and Pops house. This was at a point when William was still unaware of the plot against him. He cared very deeply about his sisters safety and viewed Vick as a threat to Pops and Leslie. William was not about to let this new boyfriend of Helen's victimize his sister in any way. William demanded that Vick leave immediately and was not shy about telling Pops how this person was scoping out all his stuff and that this new boyfriend, that nobody knew from Adam should not be up in their house and wanted to force him to leave. But for some reason, Leslie and Pops didn't want this person that they had never met before to leave.

The relationship between Vick and Helen didn't last very long. To William, it was a very suspicious situation.

About a year and a half after William became aware that his family was trying to murder him, William happened to spot Vick at local hotel. William, with his hands balled into fists ran at Vick with the intention of putting a fist or two down this murderer's throat, but as William got close, Vick dropped to one knee and covered his face with one arm and put the other one up like a traffic cop, saying, "whoa, wait a minute, whoa, whoa!"

William stood over this man, hands still balled into fists and said to him, "do you realize what those fucking people were trying to do to me!!!"

Vick responded, in an almost nonchalant tone, "yeah, I know they were trying to murder you, and man I'm sorry about that. They were trying to have you committed to the nut house also."

And then, with one of his balled up fist raised, William screamed, "WHY!!!"

Still covering his face with one arm, Vick answered, "because you inherited something when your father died"

Again, with his fist raised, William screamed, "what, what did I inherit?"

Still covering his face, Vick said, " I don't know, they wouldn't tell me. Hey, please know that, that is the reason I left."

William now lowered and unclenched his fist, and said, "they asked you to do it, didn't they?"

The look on Vicks face, the look of distraught, despair, and mostly fear, told William several things.

#1 Vick was telling William the 100% truth

#2 It is now an undeniable FACT, that William's family was really trying to murder him for some inheritance he was never told about.

#3 Vick did William solid by refusing to agree to end William's life.

Vick finally answered, "man William, you got to know that I can't answer that question, the fact that I'm not with Helen anymore should give you your answer, I mean look, I got my kids back, and got back with their mom, I'm trying to do right with my life, help me out here, I really don't want to be involved"

And it was true, William could see a woman with her hands on her hips and two young children running around behind her.

William said to Vick, "you know, I believe your telling me the truth, fuck, come here man."

William held his arms open and gave this man a hug, saying, "thanks, brother, I love you man"

Vick hugged William back, and Vick was sobbing when he said, "I'm glad you made it, thank God you survived."

William said, "yeah, you know your right, thank God I survived."

Vick said, "you got to know, I love you too, man."

The conversation ended with William saying, "I do now."

May God truly bless this man for doing the right thing, and walking away. And this proves without a shadow of a doubt that the California department of corrections CAN AND DOES rehabilitate offenders.

CHAPTER FORTYTHREE

The fear, William just had his trust in the whole world literally ripped right out of his soul. In William's mind, if his own family was desperately trying to murder him, then its extremely possible that friends and complete strangers are very capable of doing much worse. Paranoia would now set deeply into William's mindset, when would they try again???

And William would hear some very scary and horrible things being said about him from some people that associate with his family. He heard from a man named Steve, who was Ted's current wife's, ex-husband. Steve told William one day at the park, "yeah, you know I heard Ted and Leslie bragging about all the nice houses, and fancy cars they were going to buy once you were gone." Not only are William's 2 brother's and 2 sisters, complete lowlifes, THEY ARE VERY DANGEROUS. If they are willing to murder a loving family member, what are they capable of doing to just friends and strangers? One of the most gut wrenching things he was told was from Vick a couple of weeks after the incident in the hotel parking lot. William's nephew, Jack, owns a hearse, and keeps it stored in his mother Leslie's backyard. Vick told William, "yeah, Jack would joke around sometimes how he couldn't wait to give his uncle William a ride to his funeral." Now that is some way out, astronomically fucked up shit. PLEASE!!! William was just as good to Jack as he was to everyone else.

As far as how he feels about his family, let's start with the person he's least upset with.

EILEEN SR

HAMMERED DOG FUCK RAT SHIT, even though this true story is mostly about her, that NAC (for those of you who don't know what that is, it's the acronym for Nothing Ass Caucasian) her name is not worth mentioning ever again, for all Eternity, and at the least for the rest of this story. Although, at the height of the danger he was in, maybe two months before Vicks confirmation, William had a dream. And in this dream, William is on a residential restoration project,

AND,….Leslie, Eileen Jr, and Helen, for whatever reason, were with William at this jobsite. The next thing that happens is Leslie gives William a small bag of gold coins, and then asked him if he would put them somewhere safe, which he does, but right before he opened the cabinet he was going to put the coins in, he spilled them. As he put dozens of coins back in the little burlap sack, William put three of the coins in his pocket. (To this day, William has never understood this part of the dream) The very next thing that happens, is a knock at the door of this home being remodeled, and when William answered the door, she tried to say something to her son. But whatever she was going to say was 100% most certainly a lie, and William didn't even give her a chance to spit it out of her dirty, foul smelling, never been cleaned mouth she doesn't deserve to have. The dream ended with William slamming that door so hard in her face, an apparition of his right arm went right through the door, and right through her face as they both faded into NEVER ENDING NOTHINGNESS, and that was the last time William ever laid eyes on his mother.

BRIAN

That person is a gun toting hip gangster wannabe, has absolutely no idea WHO he is!!! Has never once had an original thought of his own. He is 100% under his mother's control. Manipulated as manipulated can get. You don't see many people, more manipulated than, Brian Smith.

Here's how this lowlife got his head start to a successful life, Brian Smith, who is now an Operating Officer of the largest soda company in the world (hey Pepsi, William doesn't care if you sue him for slandering, if you employ niggers like BILL SCHINK, then you're a nigger company too, and all your products suck!!!) Used to use that 45 cal. Gun, way back when he was groomed to own it, to rob honest, hardworking, GOD FEARING farmworkers of tens of thousands of dollars, and defends his actions with his anti-Semitic beliefs. That's right Pepsi, he just might try an rob you someday.

EILEEN JR

Trigger man, all five Smith children were nothing more than tools that were created by someone so utterly and grotesquely EVIL, most people reading this story can barely comprehend it.

They were just tools created to feed a gambling habit, and when they were no longer needed, just thrown away, like they were nothing. They weren't human to her, her own children, to her they were completely disposable, JUST A MEANS TO AN END!!!

HELEN SMITH

Will probably go to her grave never realizing how close she came to losing her life.

JACK DANBURY (Williams nephew, and Helen's half brother)

If I (this author) had ever said something as ugly as Jack said about his uncle, I would fully expect God to RIP my tongue out, long before he sent me to hell.

TED SMITH

For the first few years of this horrifying nightmare, William was in complete denial when it came to his older brothers involvement. First impressions go a long way, like decades long. William didn't want to believe that this was the same brother, that 40+ years ago, rescued William from a trip to the hospital. William was 7 years old at the time, on a Saturday morning. He was in a New York city school yard alone when a group of teenagers were planning to jump William and hurt him real bad. By some miracle, Ted had found out just in time about his little brothers impending doom, and was able to make it to that schoolyard and send all 5 of those punks, scrambling over an eight foot fence. William just didn't want to believe it was that same brother that set him up to be murdered.

And if that wasn't bad enough, Ted has information that would put both Eileen's and Leslie in prison for the rest of their lives.

LESLIE

This one is huge, the level of betrayal William suffered at the hands of this woman, is like when something is priceless, this level of betrayal is immeasurable, you can't even put a label on it. She literally destroyed William emotionally. She knows good and well how much her little brother loved her. William would have given his life to save hers if it had ever come to that, just to find out one day that the love William believed his sister had for him was just an elaborate illusion, a mirage in the middle of this desert called the San Joaquin Valley. The emotional pain was a <u>shank</u> shoved into the very core of Williams soul. Shame on that woman.

CHAPTER FORTYFOUR

The authorities

The night Eileen Jr all but admitted to William that she murdered their father, William started a campaign to get law enforcement to at the very least, investigate his claims, but his attempts made William feel like he was in bizzaro world. Every time William shopped a law firm, the firm acted like they were interested at first, then it seemed like after whatever little investigation of theirs was done, any and all communication stopped. Not one of the dozens lawyers William contacted couldn't even respond "yes, there is something to look into", or "no there is nothing to look into." It was the same with law enforcement. William has submitted a tip about the 10+ plus felonies that "person" is guilty of 5 DIFFERENT TIMES, TO THE FBI and got absolutely no response. William even went to the trouble of traveling to the nearest FBI field office, stripped down, not one thing in his pockets besides his California driver's license, not even a belt, out of respect for that organization, just to be told that he didn't have anything of "investigative value", how does a story about a murder conspiracy as huge as this one have no investigative value? Has the FBI become such a worthless organization that they just ignore the unwritten rule that the truth is stranger than fiction??? This author firmly believes Steven Wray is a real life ROBOT, Most people that have ever heard him speak, would probably agree.

The FBI let William in their building, and when William reached the door that led to their offices, was told basically to just go away. William walked away from that building that day completely crushed. An unimaginable feeling of loneliness, so alone in this world, the cops won't even talk to him, it was almost like he didn't even exist.

There is a possible explanation for this very immature silent treatment William has been subject to at the hands of LAZY law organizations and LAZY law enforcement.

That "person" never divorced William's father for her "important" reasons. One was so she would remain "next of kin" and retain control over this inheritance , it's not hers, she just holds it in a kind of limbo. Second, she is not legally obligated to tell William he inherited anything, and its VERY POSSIBLE "SHE" went to great lengths to make William out to be some kind unreasonable, un-responsible, ugly, violent person not worthy of any comforts in life.

THAT IS 100% NOT TRUE!!!

I know William personally, and that man is a caring, loving, generous, trying to leave the world better than he found it type of person. Has not one foul bone in his body. And he can produce HUNDREDS of credible witnesses that will swear on the bible that, that is the truth.

CHAPTER FORTYFIVE

William has a deeply profound understanding that it was Devine intervention that spared his life during the many attempts by his family to end it. And now has an even more profound appreciation for this life the creator, the GOD of his own understanding has been so kind to let him live.

AND WILL CONTINUE TO DO THE BEST HE CAN, WITH THE ABILITY'S AFFORDED TO HIM BY THE ONE TRUE LIVING GOD, to leave this world just a little better than he found it. And do it alone if he has to, right there in that red light district, in that thick town, in sunny Central California. Thank you for listening, sometimes it's all a person needs, is someone else in this world, even if it's just one other person, to hear them and make them feel that their not alone in this struggle that life can sometimes be

AMEN

AUTHORS NOTES,

Not in this life, the next life, or any other conceivable reality, did Charles Smith and William Smith deserve that level of evil put on them, not even close.

Additionally, it's a mathematical certainty that close to a 100 people in this large community, this hick town knew that several innocent people were being victimized. These people that had intimate knowledge of the crimes you were just made aware of and WERE MORALLY OBLIGATED TO DO SOMETHING, ANYTHING TO PREVENT SOME OF IT FROM HAPPEN-ING! But no one did anything but hope to get their cut. Everyone of those people should be ashamed of themselves.

William wants the whole world to know exactly how he feels about this inheritance, these assets that surely originated somewhere in Europe. What about the community where these assets are physically located, what about the people of that community that have made only GOD knows what kinds of sacrifices, with tears, sweat, and BLOOD!!! What about them??? Do they have everything they need??? Does anybody in this whole big giant shithole of a world even care??? Well, William does, and cares not what anyone thinks about it.

And now, As William would put in his style of talk, " hey Johnny law, yeah you, every single one of you, from Steve Wray to the lowest ranking cadet, and all the pigs in between, should hang their heads in shame because of everything "that person" got away with. Made you lazy motherfucker's look like just that, LAZY MOTHERFUCKER'S, thanks for nothing. Made a mockery of everything good, God fearing people believe about life. As a matter of fact, "that person" is still at this very moment, victimizing innocent people. Somehow she is getting away with a law suit against a subsidiary of Bethlehem Steel a company Charles retired from 12 years before she murdered him. Her last boy friend, Brad "died" less than a year after Charles, and she, at this very moment lives in Brad's house, with Brad's youngest daughter, a person William personally heard Brad disown, TWICE.

As far as William is concerned, because some lowlife lawyer was able to draw up a document that gave an inheritance that belongs to William, to someone else altogether, BEFORE IT WAS EVEN HIS, means that lawyer not only shit right on top of justice, but literally flushed it down the toilet.

And once again, in stark contrast to the previous statement, William would like to extend extreme gratitude to almost all of the people that live in Parkside, California, if it was not for these people, people William claims are the only family he's ever truly known, this piece of literature, would never have been brought into existence.

But above all else, two things, the main purpose of this story was to praise his father,

WILLIAM CHARLES SCHINK

He was not a good man, he was a great one, GOD speed old man.

AND.......

DONNA LYNNE TOBY

This woman is one of the most bad ass bitches to ever walk this earth. She survived one of the most horrifying victimizations anyone on earth has ever faced, and anyone that has suffered through it will agree. Donna's first born child was kidnapped over 40 years ago, and was never found.

If it was not for Donna's undeniable, unwavering, deeply profound, authentic, and most of all UNCONDITIONAL LOVE for William, not only would this story never have been told, his life would have ended that fateful day in the park, he will forever and always love, Donna Lynne Toby.

AND FINALLY, William would like to quote the GREAT, one and only, DAVE GROEL, from a song called "monkey wrench"…

ONE LAST THING BEFORE I QUIT, I NEVER WANTED ANYMORE THAN I COULD FIT INDIDE MY HEAD, I STILL REMEMBER EVERYTHING, OF WHAT YOU SAID, AND ALL THE SHIT THAT SOMEHOW CAME ALONG WITH IT, STILL THERE'S ONE THING THAT COMFORTS ME, SINCE I WAS CAGED BUT NOW I'M FREEEEE!!!!!!!!!!!!

DON'T WANT TO BE YOUR MONKEY WRENCH!!!